USING AND TROUBLESHOOTING
THE MC68000

USING AND TROUBLESHOOTING THE MC68000

JAMES WILLIAM COFFRON

RESTON PUBLISHING COMPANY, INC.

A Prentice-Hall Company
Reston, Virginia

Library of Congress Cataloging in Publication Data

Coffron, James.
    Using and troubleshooting the MC68000.

    Includes index.
    1. Motorola 68000 (Computer)   I. Title.
QA76.8.M6895C63   1983   001.64   82-16593
ISBN 0-8359-8158-4
ISBN 0-8359-8159-2 (pbk.)

Editorial supervision by
Ginger Sasser DeLacey.

© 1983 by
Reston Publishing Company, Inc.
A Prentice-Hall Company
Reston, Virginia

10   9   8   7   6   5   4   3   2   1

Printed in the United States of America

For my family
Carol, Kellese, Jeffrey and Rocky

CONTENTS

PREFACE

This book is about the 16-bit microprocessor. More specifically, it is about the 68000. Written for those who work with hardware, the book provides information and details concerning the organization of a typical 68000 system, how the 68000 controls the system, and how to "debug" and troubleshoot the system with a minimum of software.

To be of real assistance to the hardware troubleshooter, it is essential for a book of this nature to confront and come directly to grips with exact details of the schematics of circuits, devices, pin numbers, and logical voltage levels at various check points. *Using and Troubleshooting the MC68000* does this.

To implement some troubleshooting strategies, one must learn software and develop a high level of expertise in its use in order to deal with hardware. This is a problem that constitutes a major obstacle for many technicians and others who already know digital hardware and who may be familiar with 8-bit microprocessor systems, but who do not know 68000 software. For this reason, and because of other advantages, *Using and Troubleshooting the MC68000* emphasizes *Static Stimulus Testing*.

Static Stimulus Testing is a technique for hardware checkout that is virtually independent of software—yet it is powerful and effective in locating hardware malfunctions. It is a simple, straightforward extension of digital techniques—already known to many—into the field of microprocessor systems. In addition, it requires standard, low-cost instruments, such as a dc voltmeter and logic probe, plus a Static Stimulus Tester which may be purchased or constructed. The Static Stimulus Tester provides operator-controlled voltage levels, 1's and 0's, at microprocessor socket pins. These logical voltage levels propagate through the system via address lines, data bus lines, and control bus lines to their points of destination at memory pins or I/O ports. Since each logical voltage level on each bus is set by the operator and remains steady until the operator changes it, plenty of time is provided to check all points along the logic path. Such checks can be made with no software knowledge whatsoever.

Chapter 1 first presents an introduction and overview of the 68000. From there, it moves on to a review of bus structures and buffers. The rest of the chapter is devoted to showing how data is read from system ROM in a 68000-controlled microprocessor system, examining how the system is organized, what control signals are required, what name is applied to each, how these signals are generated, and what signal sequences must be observed.

In Chap. 2, we discuss the essential details of using static RAM with the 68000. Topics covered are the generation of memory control signals, select lines, and control lines, as well as a presentation and discussion of the sequence of electrical events that must take place to accomplish a memory READ or a WRITE operation. A complete schematic of the hardware involved serves as the reference of focus for the discussion.

Chapter 3 covers the same type of details as Chap. 2, but with reference to reading and writing to an I/O device rather than RAM.

Chapter 4 continues with I/O and shows how to interface the 6800-type peripheral devices to the 68000.

Chapter 5 introduces the concept of Static Stimulus Testing and examines the makeup of a Static Stimulus Tester (SST) for the 68000. A detailed discussion follows of what the SST must accomplish and the necessary hardware. The chapter closes with a summary of SST hardware.

Chapters 6, 7, and 8 concentrate on troubleshooting various aspects of the 68000 system. These chapters continue the discussion begun in Chap. 5, showing exactly how Static Stimulus Testing is used to test, troubleshoot, and verify hardware operations with software. This answers an urgent and long-standing question: How can hardware be checked, debugged, and verified in the absense of software, or prior to the development of software?

The book closes with a discussion in Chap. 9 of how to implement a "march pattern" for rapid checking of memory cells. This is a memory system diagnostic based on software. The key here is speed. However, such a technique cannot be used if too little memory and system hardware is operable to permit the program to run. So, sufficient memory space and hardware is first verified by Static Stimulus Testing to permit the march pattern diagnostic to run. Unless the necessary amount of hardware is operational, it is pointless to attempt to install a software-based diagnostic because it will invariably fail.

The discussion in Chap. 9 rounds out a troubleshooting strategy that will effectively resolve the vast majority of hardware problems in a typical 68000 microprocessor system. The future use of 16-bit devices is predictable. The fact that knowledgeable people will be needed to debug, troubleshoot, and maintain such systems is also predictable, and this means opportunity for those who can perform such jobs.

JAMES W. COFFRON

*I would like to thank
Ginger DeLacey
for her help
in the preparation of this manuscript.*

CHAPTER 1

READING DATA FROM SYSTEM ROM WITH THE 68000

1-1: INTRODUCTION

This book deals with the very real problem of how to use, troubleshoot, debug, or isolate faults in the hardware that makes up a typical 68000 microprocessor system. No matter what name you may associate with the act of locating the exact malfunction site in a microprocessor system, every experienced troubleshooter will agree that it can be a frustrating and time-consuming process. This book is written to provide the needed guidelines to anyone who is interested in effectively troubleshooting systems designed around the 16-bit 68000 microprocessor.

The book is not intended to be a hardware design manual. However, many examples of interfacing the 68000 CPU will be given and explained. These discussions are meant to serve as a guide for the person encountering a 16-bit microprocessor for the first time and will also help the beginner who is trying to learn microprocessor hardware organization or hardware troubleshooting. The intent of all such discussions is to assist you in becoming familiar with how the 68000 performs its various hardware functions. By becoming acquainted with the operating principles, sequences, and details presented in these examples, you can establish familiar ground to be called upon later when examining a new system for the first time.

The second half of the text focuses on troubleshooting. A detailed discussion of that topic cannot be undertaken until some facts concerning 68000 operation are given. Knowing these facts will allow one to follow logically each step in the troubleshooting process. To supply a solution to a problem without making certain that the elements of the problem are understood will never convince anyone of the validity of the technique shown. Thus, the first half of this text is devoted to interfacing the 68000 to all the major hardware that would be encountered in a typical 68000 system.

It may come as a surprise that the effective troubleshooting of microprocessor systems hardware does not require extensive software knowledge. We make this claim now, at the beginning of the text. You may or may not agree with it. But, by the end of this text, we challenge you to read that sentence again and decide if our claim is true. Software for the 68000 will not be emphasized in this text. Discussions of hardware troubleshooting will be made without reference to system software wherever possible. Exceptions will occur in cases where software test routines are used.

If we are to troubleshoot without using software, a new hardware debugging technique will have to be used. The technique must make hardware debugging independent of the system software. Such a technique is called *Static Stimulus Testing*. It is the main troubleshooting method used in this book. A detailed discussion of Static Stimulus Testing (SST) and how it is used will be the main focus of the latter chapters.

In cases where SST will not provide all of the troubleshooting aid that may be needed to solve a problem completely, other techniques will be given. In the debugging of system RAM, for example, Static Stimulus Testing can be used to troubleshoot all of the memory hardware. However, if the memory is large, a software memory test routine can be employed to speed the fault isolation process.

Keep in mind that the techniques for interfacing and troubleshooting described in this text are meant only as guides. Usually, you will read about a particular technique and then adjust, modify, and tailor the technique to suit the individual system requirement and your own personal preference. The goal of this book is to provide enough information to enable you to apply the techniques and troubleshoot a malfunctioning 68000 microprocessor system.

A final word: Any discussion of system troubleshooting and interfacing leaves one emptyhanded unless the discussion involves actual problems encountered in practice. To that end, each useful hardware debugging technique mentioned will be discussed in detail. Further, we will use a typical 68000 system and show how the troubleshooting techniques can be employed. Our discussion of troubleshooting will cover every major circuit of the system hardware. In this way, you will have several actual examples of how to use the troubleshooting techniques and how to interface 68000 system hardware.

1-2: OVERVIEW OF THE 68000 CPU

This section opens the technical discussion with some essential details and comments related to the 68000 microprocessor. The discussion assumes that you have some familiarity with at least one 8-bit microprocessor. If you have written some software and worked through the details of the hardware for any microprocessor system, this will be sufficient background to utilize this text profitably.

It would not be in the best interest of learning to present at this time the entire block diagram of the 68000 microprocessor. To make it easier, we will examine only those sections of the 68000 that will enhance the topic under discussion. There are many details that are extremely important to know, but you must be given enough introduction and time to appreciate them. This text will cover all of the major points for the hardware of the 68000, but they will be explained one piece at a time. The discussion is structured so that at each step you will be able to relate the new information to details already understood. In this way, you will NOT be forced to accept on faith certain facts of the 68000 operation, since other related underlying details will be known.

Figure 1-1 shows the general grouping of the 68000 physical pins. Referring to Fig. 1-1, it may not be clear to you at this time why the signals are grouped as shown. Further, you may not fully understand the names given to the signals. Each of these major

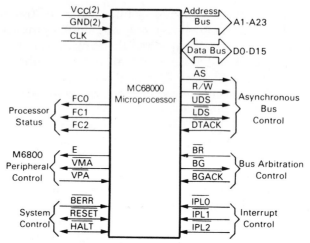

FIGURE 1–1.   Grouping of the 68000 physical pins into functional sets. (Courtesy of Motorola, Inc. © 1981)

groups will be discussed as we progress through the text at a time when it is necessary to understanding in a particular topic under consideration.

In examining the signals shown in Fig. 1-1, some of the groups are very familiar from one's knowledge of 8-bit microprocessors—for example, the group labeled "*address bus.*" There are 23 physical address lines in this group. The *data bus* group has 16 physical lines instead of 8. It is from the data bus group that the 68000 is placed into the category of 16-bit microprocessors.

The power supplies for the 68000 are +5 volts and ground. A single external clock input is used for the 68000. There is no internal clock generator on this device as in some of the 8-bit microprocessors. The electrical nature of the clock input line will be discussed later in this text.

In Fig. 1-1, there is a group of signals labeled "*Interrupt Control.*" These inputs will provide the physical means to interrupt the microprocessor. The term *interrupt* is not new and is the same as for 8-bit microprocessors.

Another group of signals shown in Fig. 1-1 is labeled "*M6800 Peripheral Control.*" These signals will be used to allow the 68000 to connect physically and to control electrically the standard 6800 peripheral devices. The 6800 is an 8-bit microprocessor and the 68000 is a 16-bit microprocessor. One of the later chapters will show how to interface the 68000 to a common 6800 peripheral device, the 6821 PIA.

Another group of 68000 signal lines shown in Fig. 1-1 is labeled *"Processor Status."* If you are used to working with the 8080, an 8-bit microprocessor, then the concept of processor status is familiar. For those readers whose background lies in other 8-bit microprocessors, the concept of processor status may be entirely new. In general, these status lines will logically indicate the type of hardware activity occurring with the 68000 at any given time.

PIN ASSIGNMENT

D4	1 ●	64	D5
D3	2	63	D6
D2	3	62	D7
D1	4	61	D8
D0	5	60	D9
$\overline{AS}$	6	59	D10
$\overline{UDS}$	7	58	D11
$\overline{LDS}$	8	57	D12
R/$\overline{W}$	9	56	D13
$\overline{DTACK}$	10	55	D14
$\overline{BG}$	11	54	D15
$\overline{BGACK}$	12	53	GND
$\overline{BR}$	13	52	A23
V_{CC}	14	51	A22
CLK	15	50	A21
GND	16	49	V_{CC}
$\overline{HALT}$	17	48	A20
$\overline{RESET}$	18	47	A19
$\overline{VMA}$	19	46	A18
E	20	45	A17
$\overline{VPA}$	21	44	A16
$\overline{BERR}$	22	43	A15
$\overline{IPL2}$	23	42	A14
$\overline{IPL1}$	24	41	A13
$\overline{IPL0}$	25	40	A12
FC2	26	39	A11
FC1	27	38	A10
FC0	28	37	A9
A1	29	36	A8
A2	30	35	A7
A3	31	34	A6
A4	32	33	A5

FIGURE 1–2. Pinout of the 68000 CPU. (Courtesy of Motorola, Inc. © 1981)

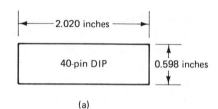

(a)

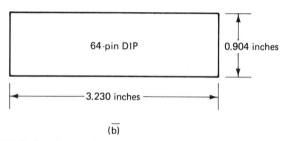

(b)

FIGURE 1–3.   Dimensions showing the difference between a 40-pin *DIP* and 64-pin *DIP*.

One fact shown in Fig. 1-1 that may also be new is the type of arrow used for two of the 68000 system control signals, *Halt and Reset.* The Halt line is shown as a bidirectional signal—that is, either the signal can originate from an external source and be sent to the 68000, or it can be output by the 68000. This is a new concept for anyone familiar with 8-bit microprocessors. In most 8-bit microprocessors, the Halt signal was unidirectional—that is, the signal originated from an external source and was sent to the microprocessor. We will be discussing most of the signals shown in Fig. 1-1 as we proceed with the interfacing examples given in this text.

Figure 1-2 shows the exact pinout of the 68000 device. It is interesting to note the size of the package in Fig. 1-2. A 68000 is packaged in a 64-pin *Dual-in-Line Package* (DIP). This package is much larger than any of the standard 40-pin DIP packages usually encountered in 8-bit microprocessors. Figure 1-3 compares the dimensions of the 64-pin DIP and the more familiar 40-pin DIP.

1-3:   68000 ADDRESS BUS

Let us now discuss how the 68000 address bus is generated in a typical system. Figure 1-4 shows the physical pinout of the 68000 address lines on the 64-pin DIP. A point to notice in this figure is

PIN ASSIGNMENT

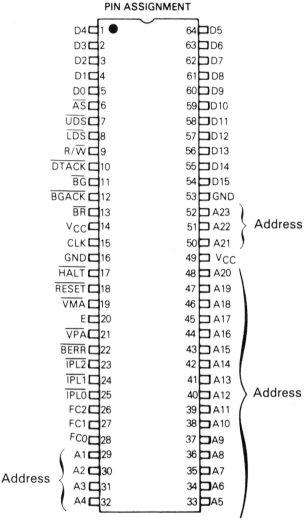

FIGURE 1–4. Physical pinout showing the address lines A1–A23. Notice that A0 is not a physical output pin on the 68000. This address line is used internally on the device. (Courtesy of Motorola, Inc. © 1981)

that the address lines start with the label "A1." Most other microprocessor devices start numbering the address line with A0.

There is a logical A0 address line on the 68000, and it is used internally on the device. The external hardware will never make use of this line. This point will become clearer as we proceed in the discussion of how to construct the physical memory space for the 68000.

All address lines A1–A23, shown in Figure 1-4, have a separate pin associated with them. This is in contrast to 16-bit microprocessors, such as the Z8000 and the 8086. Each of these microprocessors multiplex the address and data bus. The multiplexing of the address and data bus helps to reduce the pin count of the physical package. This fact allows the Z8001 to be packaged in a 48-pin DIP, while the Z8002 and the 8086 are packaged in a 40-pin DIP.

Computing the total address space for the 68000 can be done in the following way: There are 24 effective address lines, A0–A23. Remember that A0 is not physically output on the device package. With 24 address lines, the total address space can be computed as 2^{24}, or 16,777,216 physical locations.

The address space we have just computed is the total number of data bytes the 68000 can access. However, the 68000 memory space is physically organized as words (16 bits, 2 parallel bytes), reducing the total physical locations to 8,388,608 words. We will discuss more about the organization of the 68000 memory space later, when we show some examples of typical memory sytems.

At this point, it is necessary to know that there are 23 physical address lines that are output on the 68000. Further, each of these lines has a unique pin on the 64-pin device—that is, the data bus and the address bus are not time-multiplexed on the 68000.

Remember, we will be introducing all of the hardware pins of the 68000 as they are needed. Therefore, do not be concerned at this time about the other physical pins of the 68000 device. It is easier to focus attention on a small set of the device pins and to understand how that small set functions. When each small set is understood, then you can put the entire system together to obtain a working, well-understood system. This is exactly what we will do in this text.

The major lines associated with the 68000 address bus are the address lines and a control signal from the 68000 labeled "$\overline{AS}$." The address lines of the 68000 are not time-multiplexed with the data bus, and in most applications there is no need to latch the address in time. The $\overline{AS}$ control line is a signal to the external hardware that an address is output on the physical address pins and all address lines are electrically stable. Figure 1-5 shows a timing relationship between the $\overline{AS}$ control signal and the 68000 address lines A1–A23.

You may wonder why an address strobe signal is even output on the 68000 if the address lines need not be latched. One reason is that some peripheral hardware in a system can make use of the fact that the address is stable on the address lines. For example, a dynamic RAM system can use the $\overline{AS}$ signal to start the $\overline{RAS}$, MUX, $\overline{CAS}$ sequence of events for controlling the memory system.

Figure 1-6 shows one technique for generating a buffered

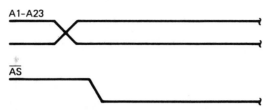

A1–A23

AS

FIGURE 1–5.   Timing diagram showing the relationship between the address lines A1–A23, and the assertion of the *AS* control line output.

memory address bus for the 68000. Notice in Fig. 1-6 that 74LS373 transparent latches are used, but the latching function is disabled. The disabling is accomplished by the Latch input to the devices being pulled up to + 5 volts via a 4.7K-ohm resistor.

In Fig. 1-6, the $\overline{\text{AS}}$ signal can be connected to the latch input pin of the 74LS373 if the designer desires. (It must be pointed out, however, that this text is not meant as a design book. The purpose of these first chapters is to give a general idea of how the hardware of the 68000 operates. This is accomplished by providing several examples of various hardware functions that may be realized with the CPU.)

Keep in mind that the information presented here is only a starting point. From this solid background, you can adapt and adjust the hardware of any particular system to better fit the chosen application. In later chapters, we will build on this foundation to show how to troubleshoot the hardware of a 68000 system easily and effectively.

Thus far, we have introduced three basic facts on the 68000 address bus. These are:

1. There are 23 physical address lines that are output on the 68000. These lines are labeled "A1–A23."
2. Each of the physical address lines has a unique pin on the 64-pin package associated with it.
3. The control signal labeled "$\overline{\text{AS}}$" is timed to give the external hardware information concerning the status of the 68000 address lines A1–A23.

1-4: 68000 DATA BUS

In this section, we will discuss the details of the 68000 system data bus. Notice in Fig. 1-7 that there are 16 physical pins for the 68000 data bus. This fact indicates that the 68000 can operate in a

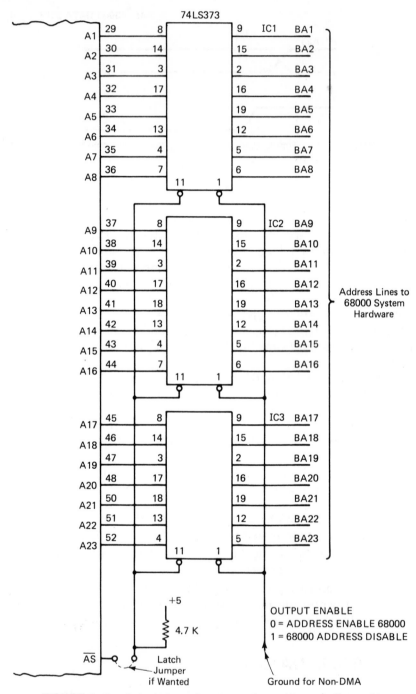

FIGURE 1–6. A technique for generating address buffers with the 68000. In this schematic, 74LS373s were used. The *AS* control signal need not be used for this buffering scheme.

PIN ASSIGNMENT

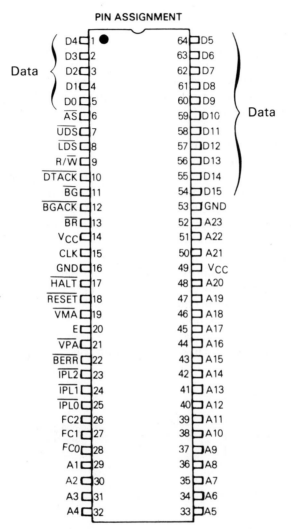

FIGURE 1–7. Physical pinout of the data lines D0–D15 on the 68000 device. (Courtesy of Motorola, Inc. © 1981)

parallel fashion on 16 physical lines of data. (Do not confuse the 16-bit data bus with the software that only performs 16-bit arithmetic operations.)

Actually, the software of the 68000 can perform operations on more than 16 bits; however, the hardware of the system can only transfer into or out of the 68000 device 16 bits at a time. For the hardware troubleshooter, this fact is extremely important. If the troubleshooter can make the 16-bit data bus perform correctly, then the software will get the required number of data words to perform the required length of operation.

Like most microprocessor devices, the data bus lines on the 68000 are bidirectional—that is, data can be transferred from the CPU to the external hardware or from the external hardware to the CPU. These operations are performed in cycles called WRITE and READ cycles. Figure 1-8 shows a block diagram of these types of data operations.

We will now introduce a new signal, which is labeled "R/$\overline{\text{W}}$," pin 9 of Fig. 1-7. This control signal is output from the 68000 and will give the electrical information regarding the type of data transfer that will occur. When the R/$\overline{\text{W}}$ line is a logical 1, the 68000 will be reading data into the device. When the R/$\overline{\text{W}}$ line is a logical 0, the 68000 will be writing data to an external device.

There are two additional signals that must be mentioned. These signals are labeled "$\overline{\text{UDS}}$ and $\overline{\text{LDS}}$," pins 7 and 8 of Fig. 1-7. The term $\overline{\text{UDS}}$ is an abbreviation for "upper data strobe" and $\overline{\text{LDS}}$ is an abbreviation for "lower data strobe." These two signals are timed control signals from the 68000. The terms "upper" and "lower" refer to the data byte of the 68000 data bus.

The 68000 data bus is 16 bits wide. These 16 bits are comprised of two parallel bytes. One byte is called the "upper byte" and the

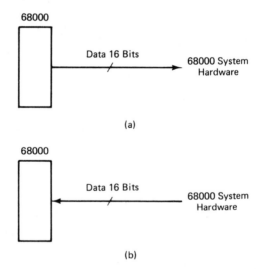

FIGURE 1–8a.   Block diagram showing the data transfer from the 68000 to the external system. This is a *WRITE* operation.
FIGURE 1–8b.   Block diagram showing the data transfer from the external hardware to the 68000. This is a *READ* operation.

other is called the "lower byte." Upper byte refers to the physical data lines D8–D15. Lower byte refers to the data lines D0–D7. Figure 1-9 shows how the upper and lower data bytes refer to the physical data pins of the 68000 data bus.

You may be asking, "Why are the two lines $\overline{\text{UDS}}$ and $\overline{\text{LDS}}$ necessary?" We will give a general answer to that question now and a more specific answer later. The 68000 is capable of communication with bytes, as well as 16-bit words. Sometimes a program is written in such a way that only the information stored in the data byte physically accessed by the bits D8–D15 may be obtained. This could be an 8-bit I/O device connected physically to these data lines (See Fig. 1-10).

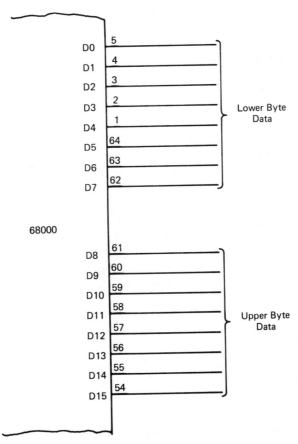

FIGURE 1–9. Diagram showing how the upper and lower data bytes refer to the physical lines of the 68000.

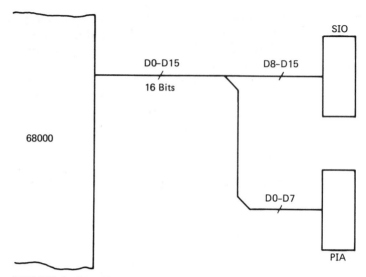

FIGURE 1–10. The 68000 can interface to 8-bit I/O devices. The devices are connected to the physical data lines on the upper or lower byte of the 68000 data bus.

In the example shown in Fig. 1-10, one may wish to READ or WRITE to the upper data byte. The software of the 68000 is such that it can control only the $\overline{\text{UDS}}$ line from the 68000 to become active during a READ or WRITE operation. In this case, the information on the lower data lines would not be electrically effected (see Fig. 1-11).

We will discuss the $\overline{\text{UDS}}$ and $\overline{\text{LDS}}$ control lines when we physically construct the microprocessor system. For now, you need to be aware that the $\overline{\text{UDS}}$ and the $\overline{\text{LDS}}$ control lines are associated with the upper data bits and the lower data bits, respectively.

In this section on the 68000 data bus, we have introduced four main points. These are:

1. There are 16 physical pins for the 68000 data bus on the 64-pin DIP.
2. The R/$\overline{\text{W}}$ control line will give electrical information as to the type of data transfer that will occur on the 68000 data bus.
3. Two control lines, $\overline{\text{UDS}}$ and $\overline{\text{LDS}}$ are associated with the upper and lower data bytes on the system data bus.
4. The 68000 can communicate with either 8 bits (upper or lower) or 16 bits at each data transfer.

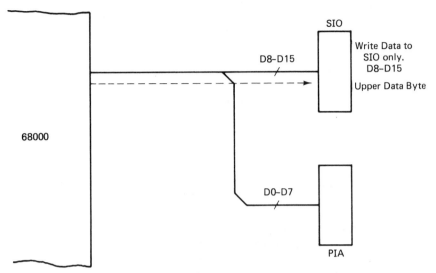

FIGURE 1–11. With I/O devices connected to both upper and lower data bytes, the 68000 can electrically communicate with either byte and not effect the I/O device on the other byte.

1-5: BIDIRECTIONAL BUFFERING FOR THE DATA BUS

Let us now discuss how the 68000 system data bus can be buffered. You are reminded that the technique shown is only one way this hardware function may be realized. The technique will work and is designed to teach the basics of bidirectional buffering for the 68000.

In later chapters, we will show exactly how to troubleshoot and verify that the bidirectional data buffers are operating correctly. If you understand how this bidirectional buffering technique operates, it will be an easy matter to understand how other techniques work.

Figure 1-12 shows a block diagram of exactly what we are going to accomplish by bidirectional buffering. In Fig. 1-12, the system data must be buffered from the external hardware to the 68000 for a READ operation. The data must be buffered from the 68000 to the external hardware for a WRITE operation.

Figure 1-13a shows the actual electrical devices that are used to realize the buffering. In Fig. 1-13a, there are two 74LS245, octal, bidirectional buffers. One of the 74LS245's buffers the upper data byte and the other buffers the lower data byte. Figure 1-13a does not show how the direction of the buffers is controlled. Figure 1-13b

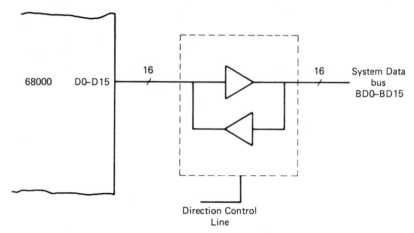

FIGURE 1–12.   Block diagram showing the concept of bidirectional buffering for the 68000 data bus.

shows a schematic diagram of how the 74LS245's are constructed internally.

The bidirectional buffers are connected in such a way that they will always enable the 68000 data pins onto the system data bus. (See Figure 1-14a.) The only time the bidirectional buffers will enable the system data onto the 68000 data pins is during a READ operation. This is done to avoid any possible "bus conflicts" with the 68000 data pins. Figure 1-14b shows a block diagram of this situation.

The 68000 control signals that will be used to provide the bidirectional buffering control are:

1. R/$\overline{\text{W}}$
2. $\overline{\text{UDS}}$ (upper data strobe)
3. $\overline{\text{LDS}}$ (lower data strobe)

We have not discussed detailed timing of these signals. For our purposes, it is not necessary to understand detailed timing. You need to know the electrical sequence of events for assertion of the control signals. The sequence of events for a READ operation is as follows:

1. The system address is output on the address lines.
2. $\overline{\text{AS}}$ is asserted.

These two events will not be of concern for our discussion on the control of the bidirectional buffers.

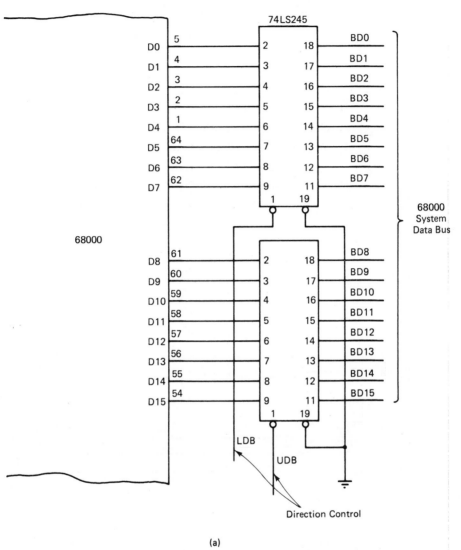

(a)

FIGURE 1–13a. Schematic diagram showing how the 74LS245 devices can be used as bidirectional data buffers.

3. Next, the R/$\overline{\text{W}}$ is set to a logical 1 if a READ operation is to occur.

4. The R/$\overline{\text{W}}$ will be set to a logical 0 if a WRITE operation will occur.

5. The upper data strobe is set to a logical 0 if the system is reading data for the upper byte or writing data for the upper byte.

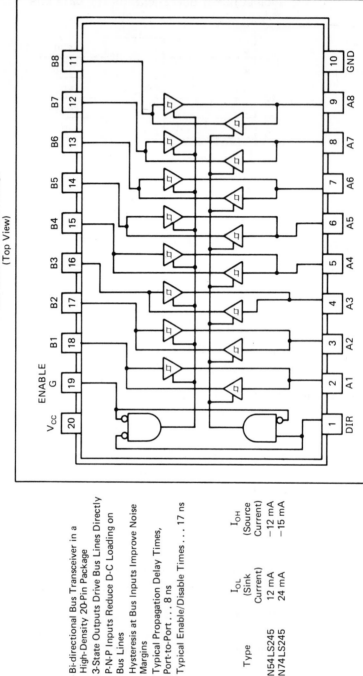

SN74LS245 . . . J Package
SN74LS245 . . . J or N Package
(Top View)

- Bi-directional Bus Transceiver in a
  High-Density 20-Pin Package
- 3-State Outputs Drive Bus Lines Directly
- P-N-P Inputs Reduce D-C Loading on
  Bus Lines
- Hysteresis at Bus Inputs Improve Noise
  Margins
- Typical Propagation Delay Times,
  Port-to-Port . . . 8 ns
- Typical Enable/Disable Times . . . 17 ns

Type	I_{OL} (Sink Current)	I_{OH} (Source Current)
SN54LS245	12 mA	−12 mA
SN74LS245	24 mA	−15 mA

(b)

FIGURE 1–13b. Functional diagram of the 74LS245 device.

18

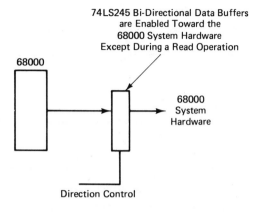

(a)

FIGURE 1–14a. Block diagram showing the fact that the bidirectional buffers are continually enabled to buffer data from the 68000 to the system except during a *READ* operation.

6. The lower data strobe is set to a logical 0 if the system is reading data for the lower byte or writing data for the lower byte.

It should be noted that both actions 5 and 6 can occur at the same time if the system is communicating in a parallel fashion with 16 bits.

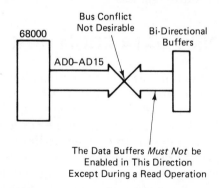

(b)

FIGURE 1–14b. Block diagram showing how a possible data bus conflict can be avoided by proper control of the bidirectional buffers.

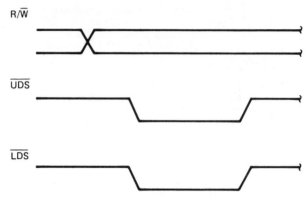

FIGURE 1–15. Timing diagram showing the relationship between the *R/W, UDS* and *LDS* control signals from the 68000.

The timing diagram of Fig. 1-15 shows the general timing for the R/$\overline{W}$, $\overline{UDS}$, and $\overline{LDS}$ signals for a byte or word communication. Using the information in Fig. 1-15, the logic can be designed for control of the bidirectional data buffers as shown in Fig. 1-16.

The bidirectional buffers (Fig. 1-16) will enable data to the 68000 only during a READ operation for either the upper data byte or the lower data byte. Remember, both bytes may be communicated with at the same time. Also, notice in Fig. 1-16 that the bidirectional buffers are continually buffering the data from the 68000 to the system data bus except during a READ operation. During a WRITE operation, the bidirectional buffers will not be affected by any of the 68000 control signals.

1-6: READING DATA FROM ROM

Enough information has been presented for us to examine how the 68000 reads data from the system ROM. The address bus and the bidirectional data bus will be involved in this hardware operation. Additional 68000 control signals will be explained as they are needed to communicate with the system ROM. Prior to a detailed discussion of how to read from ROM, it will be helpful to discuss some general concepts of accessing data in a ROM. From this general discussion, the details of exactly how the 68000 will read data from ROM will be more easily seen and understood.

The type of ROM that will be discussed is really an EPROM (Eraseable Programmable Read Only Memory). These will be 2716 devices, as shown in Fig. 1-17. The 2716 is organized as 2K $\times$ 8 bits.

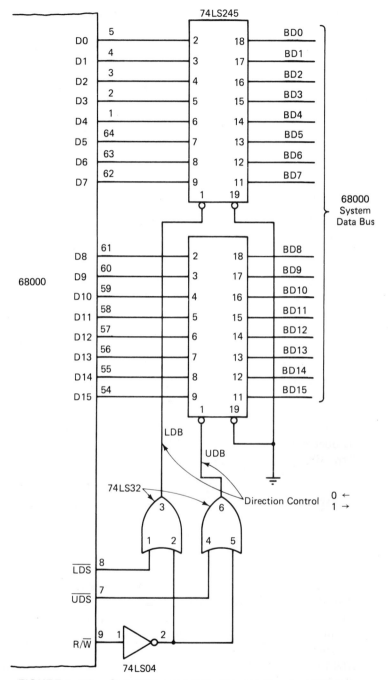

FIGURE 1–16. Complete schematic showing the electrical technique for bidirectional data buffering with the directional control logic.

PIN OUT

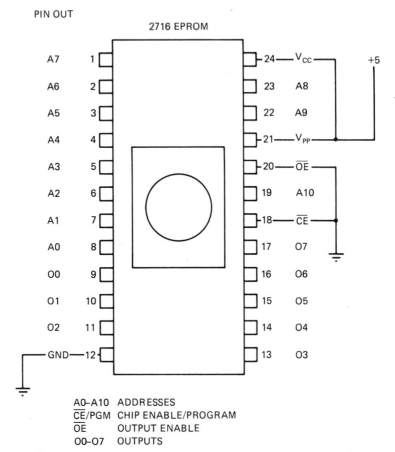

2716 EPROM

A0–A10 ADDRESSES
$\overline{\text{CE}}$/PGM CHIP ENABLE/PROGRAM
$\overline{\text{OE}}$ OUTPUT ENABLE
O0–O7 OUTPUTS

FIGURE 1–17.   Pinout diagram of the 2716 *EPROM* device. The device is connected to have data read from it.

This device is a general-purpose EPROM and many ROMs are similar in their operating characteristics for assessing internal data—therefore, the generality of the discussion will not be lost by specifying this device. In order for any microprocessor to read data from the 2716 EPROM, an address must be input to the device's memory address lines A0–A10. The $\overline{\text{CE}}$ input pin 18 must be a logical 0 and the $\overline{\text{OE}}$ input pin 20 must be a logical 0. The VPP, pin 21, is connected to + 5 volts. (See Fig. 1-17.)

Under these input conditions to the EPROM, the outputs 00–07 will be active. In a microprocessor system, the outputs of the ROM will be electrically placed on the system data bus when the microprocessor reads data from the ROM address space. This means that the 2716 outputs must drive the entire load of the system data bus. In a small system application where the data bus loading is not great, the 2716 need not be buffered before being connected to the system data bus. A rule of thumb to follow when deciding if the ROM memory system needs buffers is this:

IF THE MICROPROCESSOR REQUIRES A BIDIRECTIONAL BUFFER, THEN THE MEMORY WILL REQUIRE AN OUTPUT BUFFER.

This holds true because the microprocessor output drive capability is approximately equal to that of most semiconductor memories.

1-7: A 68000 ROM READ

Now let us examine how the 68000 reads data from the system ROM space. The 68000 has the electrical capability to read or write a single byte (8 bits) or a word (16 bits) during each READ or WRITE operation. The system memory is organized as N × 16 bits, where N is the number of unique address locations. When the 68000 reads data from memory, the system memory hardware need not be electrically informed whether a byte or a word is to be read. The system hardware can simply place the entire 16 bits on the data bus and let the microprocessor read the data it requires. (Refer to Fig. 1-18.)

When the microprocessor reads the most significant byte of data from ROM, D8–D15, the memory address is an even number.

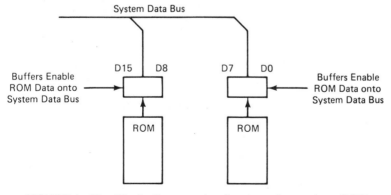

FIGURE 1–18. Block diagram showing how the system *ROM* places data on the system data bus via the memory buffers.

Stated another way, D8–D15 will be read from an address where A0 is a logical 0. Data bits D0–D7 will be read from an odd-numbered address, or an address where A0 is a logical 1. The system software will logically call for the hardware to output an odd or even address when the 68000 is performing operations using data bytes. Recall that address bit A0 is used internally on the 68000 to generate the $\overline{\text{UDS}}$ and $\overline{\text{LDS}}$ output control signals.

A question that may arise at this time is, "When the 68000 reads a word, 16 bits, from memory, does it use two memory READ operations? One with A0 set to a logical 0 and the other with A0 set to a logical 1?" The answer to that question is "No." The 68000 can and does read all 16 bits in a single memory READ operation. The internal logic of the 68000 will let the $\overline{\text{UDS}}$ and the $\overline{\text{LDS}}$ signals become asserted at the same time when reading 16 bits.

For now, it is assumed that all memory READ operations from system ROM will be word (16-bit) operations. This assumption is valid for ROM and does not impose any restrictions on the system performance.

When reading all words from the system ROM address space, the internal address line A0 is electrically ignored by the 68000. The UDS and LDS will become asserted at the same time. Address lines A1–A11 are used as the address inputs for the 2716. We will use system address lines A12–A15 for the generation of memory select lines. Certain 68000 control bits are combined logically to provide the memory data buffer enable line control. A schematic diagram for a 4K × 16-bit ROM system for the 68000 is given in Fig. 1-19.

Referring to Fig. 1-19, it should be noted that the address space 0000–0FFF is provided by ROMs A, B. The memory space 1000–1FFF is provided by ROMs C, D. All 23 address lines are logically defined for the 68000 at each memory operation. We are using only 15 of the total lines in this example. It appears from the mapping of the address space that it is in 4K blocks, making the total address space equal to 8K. We stated that the decoded space was to be used by 2716's which are organized as 2K × 8 bits.

The answer to this seeming inconsistency is that the 68000 memory space is referenced to a byte organization. A byte organization requires that the CPU use twice the address space afforded by a single byte if it is to communicate with a memory that is 16 bits wide.

It can further be seen from Fig. 1-19 that the A0 bit of the address bus is electrically ignored. This may be inferred by the fact that this pin is not output by the 68000. Therefore, the memory

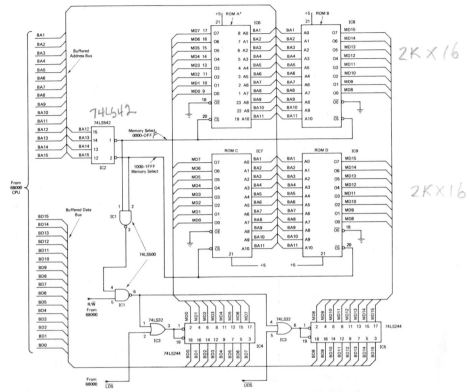

FIGURE 1–19. Complete schematic of a 4K × 16 *ROM* system for a 68000.

capacity of the 68000 is 16 *megabytes* or 8 *megawords*. In the memory schematics shown in later chapters, you are asked to recall this fact concerning the memory space allocation. The memory decoding will appear to allow twice the needed address space for the memory, but keep in mind that the address space has the required number of bytes that are decoded.

The key to understanding the ROM system of Fig. 1-19 is in noting that the 68000 sets up certain electrical conditions by the use of its address and data and control bits. When the electrical conditions are correct, a reliable signal path is established from the ROM output lines to the 68000 data input pins. There is a source of data (ROM), a destination for data (68000 CPU), and a complete path for data in which the necessary hardware has been enabled.

To further emphasize this point, let us go through the sequence of electrical events for a memory READ operation. All through the sequence of events there will be no mention of exact timing. The signal relationships will be discussed as individual electrical events. Some events will occur before others, while other events will occur at the same time. General timing diagrams will be used to emphasize and verify this point about sequence. Hardware response to the sequence of events will be given. To follow our discussion, the schematic of Fig. 1-19 will be studied as well as Figs. 1-6 and 1-16.

1-8: SEQUENCE OF ELECTRICAL EVENTS FOR A MEMORY READ

The following list of events is the general sequence that the 68000 will execute when performing a memory READ operation. (It should be noted that certain 68000 device outputs will not be mentioned. These outputs will be changing electrically during a memory READ operation but are left out of the discussions at this time. They will be introduced later, as they are needed.) Only the 68000 outputs that will directly affect the hardware operation under consideration will be mentioned. Note, also, that these electrical events occur rapidly—sometimes measured in hundreds of nanoseconds—giving the illusion of dynamic operation. However, for understanding and troubleshooting, these events can be slowed down and treated as static electrical events.

1. First, the microprocessor device lines A1–A23 will have the memory address output on them.

Referring to Fig. 1-6, we see that the inputs to the 74LS373's will become active with the system address inputs. Note that the address is now present at the 74LS373 output lines. If the $\overline{AS}$ line is used, the address will still be present at the outputs due to the active edge of the latch control for the 74LS373.

2. Next, the R/$\overline{W}$ output line from the 68000 will go to a logical 1, indicating that the system is performing a READ operation.

This action will force the input pin 5 of the 7400 NAND gate in Fig. 1-19 to a logical 1.

3. The $\overline{AS}$ signal goes to a logical 0, under the control of the 68000.

The address information on the 68000 device pins A1–A23 is now latched at the 74LS373 outputs. This action will occur only if the $\overline{AS}$ output line has been connected to the latch enable input of the 74LS373's shown in Fig. 1-6. If this is not the case, then the $\overline{AS}$ output line from the 68000 will have no effect on the overall memory communication.

With the address lines A1–A23 becoming valid to the memory system, the 2716 address input lines A0–A10 have active inputs. The 74LS42 decoder shown in Fig. 1-19 has address output lines BA12–BA15 applied to its inputs. Let us suppose that the 68000 is reading from memory address 0400 in hexadecimal notation. Under these conditions, output pin 1 of the 74LS42 will be an active 0. With pin 1 an active 0, the $\overline{CS}$ input to the 2716 pin 20 of ROMs A and B will be active.

When the $\overline{CS}$ input to ROMs A and B becomes active, the ROM outputs are enabled onto the memory data bus lines MD0–MD15. These ROM outputs are not enabled onto the system data bus lines at this time. MD0–MD15 refer to the memory data lines at the input to the data buffers IC4 and IC5 of Fig. 1-19.

4. The $\overline{UDS}$ and $\overline{LDS}$ outputs from the 68000 are asserted to a logical 0.

When this action occurs, the 68000 is electrically informing the external hardware that it is ready to receive data. Figure 1-19 shows the $\overline{UDS}$ and the $\overline{LDS}$ connected to different inputs of a 74LS32 OR gate, IC3. When the memory space is enabled via pin 6 of the 74LS00 and the $R/\overline{W}$ signal is a logical 1, input pins 1 and 4 of the 74LS32 OR gates are enabled to a logical 0.

Memory data buffers IC4 and IC5 are not enabled until the $\overline{UDS}$ or the $\overline{LDS}$ timed control signal from the 68000 is asserted. If the 68000 is reading data from the upper data byte, the $\overline{UDS}$ is asserted. With $\overline{UDS}$ becoming asserted, output pin 6 of the 74LS32 OR gate, IC3, is set to a logical 0.

With pin 6 becoming a logical 0, the 74LS244 data buffer, IC5, is enabled. Now the data from the 2716 EPROM (ROM B) is enabled onto the system data bus lines BD8–BD15.

If the 68000 sets the timed control signal $\overline{UDS}$ to a logical 0, output pin 3 of the 74LS32 OR gate, IC3, is set to a logical 0. The memory data buffer, IC4, is now enabled onto the system data bus via input pins 1 and 19. With the 74LS244 becoming enabled, memory data from the EPROM (ROM A) is placed onto the system data bus lines BD0–BD7.

From the preceding discussion, it can be seen that either the upper memory data byte or the lower memory data byte can be electrically placed on the system data bus, regardless of the state of the other byte. Further, if the software of the 68000 directs the CPU to communicate with an entire word on the data bus, both the $\overline{\text{UDS}}$ and the $\overline{\text{LDS}}$ output control lines are asserted. Thus, both of the 74LS244's, IC4 and IC5, are enabled. When this occurs, the data from the EPROM (ROM A and ROM B) will be placed on the system data bus lines BD0–BD15.

It should be noted that if the system EPROM space is designed such that byte data will never be accessed, then it is possible to eliminate the need for selecting the upper or lower byte. Whenever the memory space is accessed, the memory data can simply be placed on the system data bus at the correct time, using all of the data bits. However, care must be taken to avoid any possible bus conflicts with the bidirectional data buffers used by the CPU.

At this point, our attention focuses on the bidirectional buffers shown in Fig. 1-16. These buffers are enabled as required to permit data from the system data bus lines BD0–BD15 to be input to the 68000 device pins D0–D15. This is accomplished by the 74LS32 OR gates in Fig. 1-16 having the input pins 1 and 4 at a logical 0 level. Pins 2 and 5 of the 74LS32 are a logical 0 due to the $R/\overline{W}$ signal becoming an active 1 and being inverted by the 74LS04. This signal indicates a READ operation.

Pins 1 and 4 of the 74LS32's are set to a logical 0 because $\overline{\text{UDS}}$ and $\overline{\text{LDS}}$ are active logical 0, indicating that the 68000 is electrically prepared to initiate the data transfer. In Chap. 2, we will see that the $\overline{\text{UDS}}$ and $\overline{\text{LDS}}$ signals are also active logical 0 during a memory WRITE operation. Notice in Fig. 1-16 that the direction control line is labeled by arrows that indicate in which direction the data is being buffered based on the logical condition of pin 1 on the 74LS245's.

During the time that all of the preceding electrical conditions are stable, there is a valid electrical path from the 2716 EPROMs A, B of Fig. 1-19 through the memory data buffers (74LS244's) onto the system data bus. From the system data bus, the electrical path is through the bidirectional buffers of Fig. 1-16. The output of these buffers is the final input to the 68000 microprocessor device pins D0–D15.

It should be noted that this path will remain stable as long as the electrical conditions just described exist. This particular point is the main focus of Static Stimulus Testing. The electrical sequence of events will be referred to when discussing troubleshooting of the 68000 memory READ operation.

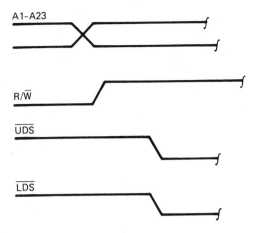

A1–A23

R/$\overline{W}$

$\overline{UDS}$

$\overline{LDS}$

All of the Above Signals are Output From
the 68000. *These* Signals Will Remain as
Shown Until DTACK Input to the 68000
is Set to A Logical 0.

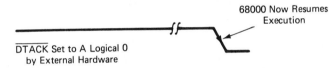

68000 Now Resumes
Execution

$\overline{DTACK}$ Set to A Logical 0
by External Hardware

FIGURE 1–20. The 68000 system signals shown will remain stable until some external hardware asserts the *DTACK* input signal to
the device.

The next event to occur in the electrical sequence will involve a
68000 input line that we have not previously discussed. That pin is
labeled "DTACK." The $\overline{DTACK}$ input pin is an abbreviation for
"*DATA TRANSFER ACKNOWLEDGE.*" The 68000 micro-
processor will keep the preceding electrical events stable on the
system buses until the external hardware responds with the information that it is electrically ready to have the 68000 strobe the
data. (Figure 1-20 shows a timing diagram representation of this
concept.)

Each data transfer from the 68000 with external hardware
must be done in a "handshake" mode. This is necessary because the
68000 is a very fast microprocessor. It can take data faster than
some memory or peripheral devices can send or receive. Therefore,
the $\overline{DTACK}$ input will allow the external device to slow down the
68000 when communicating with it.

In the next chapter, we will show how to slow down the 68000
by making use of this input pin. For now, let us assume that the

68000 is running at a sufficiently slow clock speed to allow enough time for memory access. In this case, we will not handshake from the system memory. The $\overline{\text{DTACK}}$ input is set to a logical 0 as soon as the $\overline{\text{UDS}}$ or the $\overline{\text{LDS}}$ output lines are asserted. (See Fig. 1-21a). Figure 1-21b shows a timing diagram representation of how the $\overline{\text{DTACK}}$ input becomes active during a memory communication.

   5. The $\overline{\text{DTACK}}$ input to the 68000 is set to a logical 0 by the external hardware.

   The 68000 will not proceed in the data transfer until the $\overline{\text{DTACK}}$ input has been set to a logical 0. When we discuss troubleshooting the 68000, we will supply techniques to verify that the $\overline{\text{DTACK}}$ input line is being set to a logical 0.

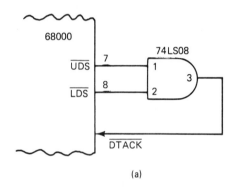

(a)

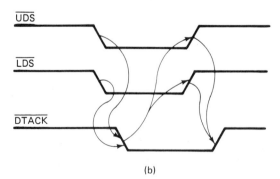

(b)

FIGURE 1–21a. Schematic diagram showing how the *DTACK* input to the 68000 will be asserted in this memory sample.
FIGURE 1–21b. Timing diagram showing the timing relationship between the *UDS, LDS,* and *DTACK* input to the 68000.

6. $\overline{\text{UDS}}$, $\overline{\text{LDS}}$, and $\overline{\text{AS}}$ signals will be set to the unasserted logical condition.

A logical 1 level is the unasserted state for these output lines. The 68000 sets these signals to a logical 1 level, indicating that the memory READ operation and the preceding sequence of events is complete. At this point, the data transfer should have occurred. The statement "should have occurred" is used because there is no way to determine directly if the data from ROM was correctly strobed into the 68000. At this point, the data transfer should have occurred. The statement "should have occurred" is used because there is no way to determine directly if the data from ROM was correctly strobed into the 68000.

The data is strobed into the 68000 after the $\overline{\text{DTACK}}$ input has been asserted by the external hardware. The rising edge of $\overline{\text{UDS}}$ or $\overline{\text{LDS}}$ is the active edge that will strobe the data into the 68000.

1-9: SUMMATION OF A MEMORY READ SEQUENCE FOR THE 68000

Let us now summarize the sequence of events that will occur in a memory READ sequence for a 68000. The sequence will be referred to later in the chapters on troubleshooting. The sequence is:

1. A1–A23 are set to a logical value of the system memory address from which the memory data will be read.
2. R/$\overline{\text{W}}$ is set to a logical 1. This indicates that a READ operation will be occurring in the system hardware.
3. $\overline{\text{AS}}$ is set to a logical 0. When $\overline{\text{AS}}$ is a logical 0, the microprocessor device lines A1–A23 are valid to the system memory space.
4. $\overline{\text{UDS}}$, $\overline{\text{LDS}}$, or both are set to a logical 0. These are the timed output control signals to the 68000 system hardware. These signals indicate that the microprocessor is electrically ready to receive data. When $\overline{\text{UDS}}$ or $\overline{\text{LDS}}$ is a logical 0, the ROM data is placed on the system data bus by the external system hardware. ROM data is then sent to the bidirectional buffer, to the 74LS245's, and finally to the input to the 68000 device pins D0–D15.
5. The $\overline{\text{DTACK}}$ input to the 68000 will be set to a logical 0 by the external hardware. This signal indicates that the external hardware is electrically prepared to continue in the memory cycle.
6. $\overline{\text{LDS}}$, $\overline{\text{UDS}}$, and $\overline{\text{AS}}$ control lines are set to a logical 1 by the

68000. This action terminates the data transfer. Data are latched internally on the 68000 on the rising edge of these signals. The ROM data are removed from the system data bus. The 68000 is now ready to perform another data transfer. The transfer can be another memory READ or any other valid hardware operation.

1-10: CHAPTER SUMMARY

This chapter has described and illustrated a number of essential points concerning the 68000 hardware operation. The function of several control bits such as $\overline{AS}$, $R/\overline{W}$, $\overline{UDS}$, $\overline{LDS}$, and $\overline{DTACK}$ were discussed. A complete schematic of a 4K × 16-bit ROM memory was shown and interfaced to the 68000.

It can be seen that many general concepts concerning microprocessor systems that were valid for 8-bit devices are equally valid for 16-bit CPUs. Some of these concepts are techniques for generating memory select lines, bidirectional data buffering, and memory buffering. A major objective of the chapter was to cover the essential details of how the 68000 reads data from the system ROM. No software that would allow the 68000 to read from system ROM was presented. Discussion centered on hardware functions, sequence of events, and circuit details. It was assumed that the microprocessor was directed to read from ROM, and when it did, this is how the hardware would operate.

Not all 68000 device pins were discussed in this chapter. Only those device pins essential for a particular hardware operation were presented. In the chapters that follow, more of the 68000 device pins will be shown, following the same scheme. As mentioned before, each new device pin will be presented in such a way that its function can be related to familiar information that has already been covered.

Chapter 2 will cover the concept of reading and writing data to the system RAM. That chapter will also make use of many concepts which have already been discussed. The reader should understand the information covered in this chapter before preceding to Chap. 2.

USING STATIC RAM WITH THE 68000

2-1: OVERVIEW OF THE SYSTEM RAM

This chapter will cover a hardware interface to static RAM using the 68000. Decoding techniques and buffering realizations used in this chapter are designed to instruct. The techniques are not meant as final solutions. This system hardware design is very straightforward; with it, you may follow how the decoding and electrical communications are accomplished. After you have seen how it can be done, steps may then be taken to minimize the package count and possibly increase system performance.

Before you can begin to design or troubleshoot the hardware for a RAM system, a block diagram of how the RAM communicates with the microprocessor must be understood. A 68000 system RAM is organized as N × 16, where N is the number of unique storage

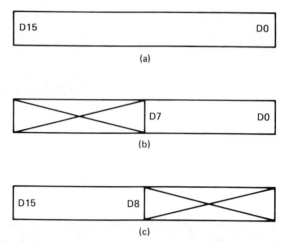

FIGURE 2–1. Block diagram showing the possible read and write combinations for *RAM* with the 68000.
a) The 68000 can read or write an entire word, 16 bits.
b) The 68000 can read or write the low byte D0–D7. The "X" indicates the high byte of *RAM* is not disturbed during this data transfer.
c) The 68000 can read or write the high byte D8–D15. During this operation, the low byte will not be disturbed.

locations of the memory. The RAM system we will design is organized as 1K × 16. Further, the RAM system can be thought of as having two separate halves, or parallel bytes. These are the upper half (D8–D15) and the lower half (D0–D7). The 68000 can read data in byte or word form, as shown in Fig. 2-1.

In Fig. 2-1, we see that one possible combination for reading and writing to the system memory is with an entire word (16 bits). In the word mode, both halves of the system memory are enabled. (See Fig. 2-2 for a block diagram of the system memory.) Another possibility for communication between the 68000 and the system memory is to read or write a byte from the upper half. (See Fig. 2-1b.) In this mode, the data bits D8–D15 will be communicated with. To select electrically the upper half of the memory, the system address must be even (A0 = 0). The third combination for communication between the microprocessor and system memory is shown in Fig. 2-1c. In this mode, the CPU will read or write data to the lower byte. For this to occur, the system address must be odd (A0 = 1). The communication will be with data bits D0–D7.

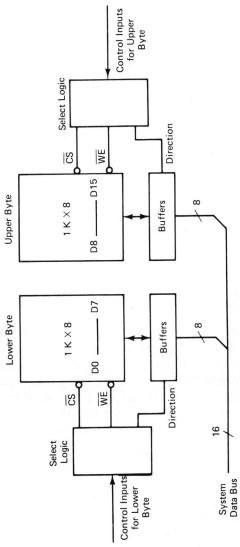

FIGURE 2–2. Block diagram of the important hardware blocks needed for electrical communication with static *RAM* for the 68000.

35

2-2:   THE MEMORY CONTROL SIGNALS

In reviewing the possible electrical events that can occur in communication with static RAM, we provide this list:

1. READ data word (D0–D15).
2. READ upper byte (D8–D15).
3. READ lower byte (D0–D7).
4. WRITE data word (D0–D15).
5. WRITE upper byte (D8–D15).
6. WRITE lower byte (D0–D7).

From this list of possible electrical events, we must design the system hardware to accomplish all of the events to occur electrically. The hardware will be designed to make use of this list and of some specific 68000 control signals. The control signals that will be used for the memory operations are:

1. $R/\overline{W}$
2. $\overline{UDS}$
3. $\overline{LDS}$

Using the list of electrical events and the 68000 control signals just mentioned, the logical conditions of the control signals for each event as seen in the truth table of Fig. 2-3 can be shown. Note that the $R/\overline{W}$ control signal used in Fig. 2-3 is not a timed control line— that is, this signal is valid for the entire memory operation. An example of a timed control signal is $\overline{UDS}$. This signal is valid or asserted for only a portion of time during the memory operation.

CPU Function	Truth Table		
	$R/\overline{W}$	$\overline{LDS}$	$\overline{UDS}$
Read Word	1	0	0
Read Upper Byte	1	1	0
Read Lower Byte	1	0	1
Write Word	0	0	0
Write Upper Byte	0	1	0
Write Lower Byte	0	0	1

FIGURE 2–3. *CPU* function list. The logical level of the 68000 outputs is shown beside the corresponding system memory operation that will take place. These logical combinations will be decoded with hardware.

The type of logic required to interface a RAM to the 68000 will be very dependent on the memory used. We will show the logic required to interface the 68000 to a memory system comprised of 2114, 1K × 4, common I/O RAM. From this disucssion, you will be able to understand better how to interface the 68000 to other types of memory devices.

2-3: GENERATION OF THE MEMORY SELECT LINES

The system static RAM resides in some predetermined address space. The address space that was chosen for this example was 3000–3FFF. The selection of this system address space was arbitrary. The RAM address space could be any available memory area in the system. When the allowed memory space for this example is examined, it is seen that 4096 memory locations are allocated. Remember, in the 68000 this means 4096 bytes; therefore, we have reserved 2048 words. Our static RAM system is organized as 2048 × 16 bits.

It was stated that the sample memory would be organized as 1K × 16. This means that not all of the available static RAM space will be used. The 2114 memories are organized as 1024 × 4. Because of this, we must further subdivide the 2K of RAM space into two separate blocks of 1K each. Figure 2-4 shows how this can be accomplished with hardware.

As shown in Fig. 2-4, the upper system address lines BA12–BA15 provide the first level of memory select—that is, they will separate the RAM space from the rest of the memory space. These address lines are the same as those that were discussed in Chap. 1. The device shown in Fig. 2-4 is a 74LS42 decoder. State 3, pin 4, is used to generate the memory space select line 3000–3FFF. The address line BA11 is used to divide the major space into two separate spaces, 3000–37FF and 3800–3FFF. The resulting memory select lines are labeled "$\overline{\text{MSELA}}$ and $\overline{\text{MSELB}}$."

In Fig. 2-4, the memory select line $\overline{\text{MSELA}}$ (3000–37FF) is active logical 0 when the following conditions exist:

1. BA15–BA12 = 0 0 1 1 (3000–3FFF) major space decode

and

2. BA11 = logical 0 (3000–37FF) minor space decode

$\overline{\text{MSELB}}$ is active logical 0 when the following conditions exist:

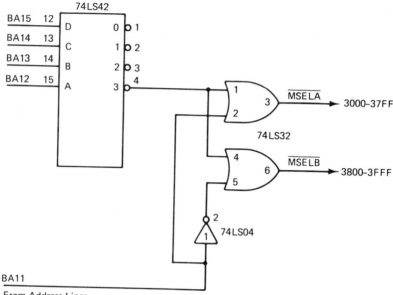

FIGURE 2–4. Schematic of the hardware necessary to decode the correct memory space during a memory transfer.

1. BA15–BA12 = 0 0 1 1 (3000–3FFF) major space decode

and

2. BA11 = logical 1 (3800–3FFF) minor space decode

We will make use of the $\overline{\text{MSELA}}$ only in the following example. The second address space 3800–3FFF will not be used.

2-4: THE 2114 COMMON I/O RAM

Generation of the exact memory control lines for any system is very dependent on the type of memory that has been selected for use in the system. The 2114, 1K × 4, common I/O static RAM was chosen for this discussion because it is in wide general use in industry. If this general discussion of how to use this device with the 68000 is understood, it will be a much easier task to transfer these details to other types of memory devices.

Let us consider the 2114 at the user level only. Further, it will be assumed that the memory access time is consistent with the overall system speed—that is, we do not need to generate any wait states for slow memory. This will be shown at the end of the chapter in a separate section. We begin by considering how many memory devices we will need for our system. Each 2114 is 4 bits wide. This will require that four 2114's be addressed in parallel to realize the entire 16-bit data word. (See Fig. 2-5.)

In order to address the memories in parallel, system address lines BA1–BA10 will be input to the 2114 address lines A0–A9. (See Fig. 2-6.) The data input and output lines will be assigned as shown in Fig. 2-6.

Let us now review how data are read from the 2114 memory. To read data from the 2114, the memory address must be input, and to enable the chip ($\overline{CS} = 0$), pin 8 needs to be active. When this occurs, the memory data output lines are active. The memory output

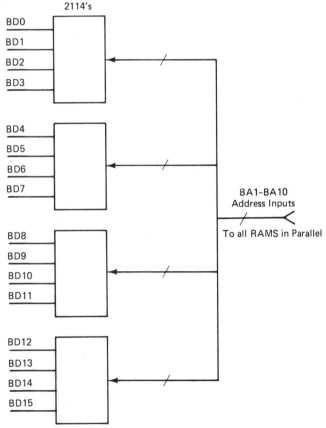

FIGURE 2–5. Block diagram showing how four 2114, 1K × 4, static *RAM* devices are placed in parallel to produce a 1K × 16 system memory.

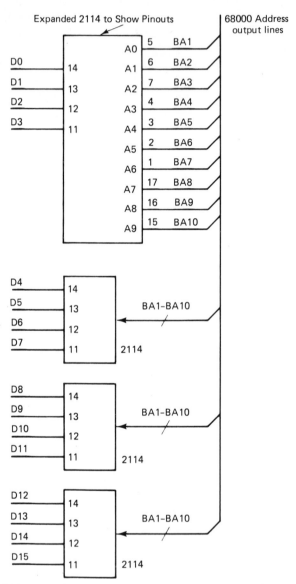

FIGURE 2–6. Schematic diagram indicating how the system's latched address lines are connected to all memory devices in a parallel fashion.

lines are multiplexed I/O. During a READ operation, the I/O lines of the memory are treated as memory data outputs. In a small system, the memory output lines can be connected directly to the system data bus. For our system, we are using memory data buffers. The 2114 data lines serve as both input and output; therefore, bidirectional buffers are used. In the ROM system of Chap. 1, unidirectional buffers were used (74LS244's) since data flow is from memory only.

The bidirectional buffers must be enabled in the correct direction when the system is reading data from the 2114. Required signal conditions are shown in Fig. 2-7. The bidirectional memory buffers will be enabled such that they are buffering data from the system data bus to the RAM except during a memory READ operation. This buffering is done so that there will be no bus conflict with the memory bidirectional buffers and the system data bus. There will be no conflict with the memory data pins because the device will not be selected except when reading or writing to it. (See Fig. 2-8.)

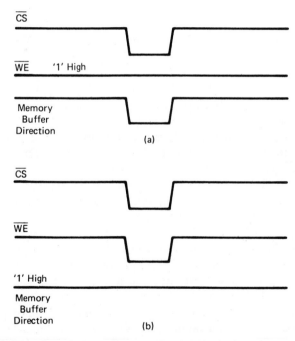

FIGURE 2–7. Timing diagram showing how the memory data buffers will be enabled during (a) a *READ* cycle, and (b) a *WRITE* cycle.

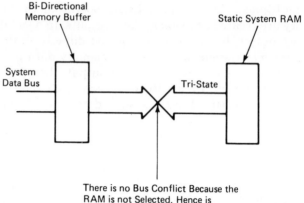

There is no Bus Conflict Because the
RAM is not Selected, Hence is
Unaffected by Signals from the Buffer

FIGURE 2–8. Block diagram of a possible bus conflict between
the 2114 data output lines and the memory data buffer outputs.
This conflict is avoided by proper control of the memory data buffer
direction control line.

From the preceding discussion, it has been shown that two
electrical operations must occur during a memory READ operation.
These are:

1. Enable the 2114's (pin 8 = logical 0).
2. Bidirectional buffers are enabled in the correct direction.

In the system under discussion, the bidirectional buffers will
be enabled in the correct direction for a memory READ operation if
the direction control line to the buffers is a logical 0.

When writing to the 2114, the data in is applied to the data
lines of the memory, and the chip enable and write enable lines are
asserted. Since the 2114's are common I/O devices, there are some
timing restrictions on the $\overline{\text{WE}}$ and the $\overline{\text{CS}}$ inputs. When writing data
to the 2114, the $\overline{\text{CS}}$ signal must not be asserted before the $\overline{\text{WE}}$ signal
is asserted because when the $\overline{\text{CS}}$ signal is asserted, the 2114 outputs
become active. If the outputs are active and the microprocessor is
sending data into the device, a bus conflict will result. (See Fig. 2-9.)

This potential problem can be eliminated by asserting the $\overline{\text{WE}}$
input and the $\overline{\text{CE}}$ input at approximately the same time. This action
is consistent with the 2114 timing specifications. Figure 2-10 shows
the timing required to realize the general functions of reading and
writing data to the 2114 memory. In Fig. 2-10, the bidirectional
buffer control is a logical 1 during a memory WRITE operation. Also

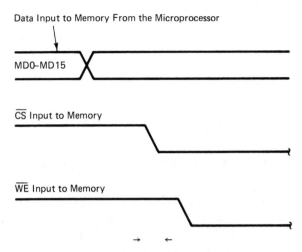

FIGURE 2–9.   Timing diagram showing the incorrect way to control the memory data buffers. In this case, there will be a bus conflict as shown in Fig. 2–8.

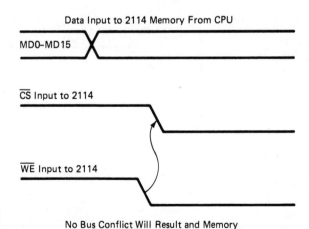

FIGURE 2–10.   Timing diagram showing the correct way to control the memory data buffers. In this instance, the bus conflict shown in Fig. 2–8 will be avoided.

shown in Fig. 2-10 are the three distinct memory control signals required for electrical communication with the 2114. These memory control signals are:

1. Chip Enable Control.
2. Write Enable Control.
3. Memory Buffer Direction Control.

2-5: THE 2114 MEMORY CONTROL LINES

The schematic for generating the memory control lines for the 2114 is shown in Fig. 2-11. The first point to note in Fig. 2-11 is that there are two almost identical circuits. The upper circuit is for generation of the upper byte memory control signals D8–D15, and the lower circuit is for generation of the lower byte memory control signals D0–D7.

The inputs to Fig. 2-11 are labeled "R/$\overline{\text{W}}$," "$\overline{\text{MSELA}}$," "$\overline{\text{UDS}}$," and "$\overline{\text{LDS}}$." These signals were discussed earlier in this text. Input

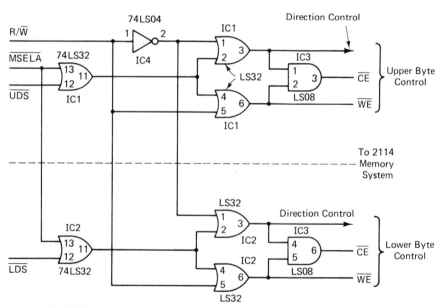

FIGURE 2–11. Schematic diagram showing how the control signals for the memory data buffer control and interface signals are generated.

line $\overline{\text{MSELA}}$ of Fig. 2-11 is the memory select output that was discussed in Fig. 2-4. Inputs R/$\overline{\text{W}}$, $\overline{\text{UDS}}$, and $\overline{\text{LDS}}$ are outputs from the 68000, with $\overline{\text{UDS}}$ and $\overline{\text{LDS}}$ being timed control outputs.

Let us examine the case where the microprocessor is reading a word (16 bits) from the system RAM. Under this condition, the inputs of the circuit of Fig. 2-11 would be:

1. R/$\overline{\text{W}}$ is a logical 1. This indicates a READ operation.
2. $\overline{\text{MSELA}}$ (Select 3000–37FF = 0) is set in the active mode.

With the inputs to Fig. 2-11 in these logical states, input pin 5 of IC1 and IC2 will be a logical 1. This logical 1 will disable the OR gates. No matter what the logical states of the other inputs to the circuit of Fig. 2-11 are, the $\overline{\text{WE}}$ control line to the upper byte or the lower byte will not become asserted. It will remain a logical 1.

The input pin 1 of IC1 and IC2 will be a logical 0. Input pin 13 of IC1 and IC2 will be a logical 0. This is due to the $\overline{\text{MSELA}}$ line and the R/$\overline{\text{W}}$ line both set to a logical 0 at the same time. With these inputs at a logical 0 level, the corresponding OR gates are enabled. When the $\overline{\text{UDS}}$ and $\overline{\text{LDS}}$ timed control lines are set to a logical 0, the output pin 3 of IC1 and IC3 will become a logical 0.

Output pin 3 of IC1 and IC3 is the buffer direction control for the upper and lower byte data. The bidirectional buffers for the upper and lower byte data will be enabled in the correct direction for a memory read. Further, output pins 3 and 6 of IC3 will be set to a logical 0. These outputs will force the $\overline{\text{CS}}$ input to the 2114's to a logical 0. The 2114's are now enabled, and data is placed on the system data bus. When the $\overline{\text{UDS}}$ and $\overline{\text{LDS}}$ timed control lines go to a logical 1, data from the 2114's is removed from the system data bus.

The electrical action just described will occur when a word (16 bits) is read from the system memory. If a byte is to be read from memory, either the $\overline{\text{UDS}}$ or the $\overline{\text{LDS}}$ timed control line will become asserted. The line that does not become asserted will remain a logical 1. Under these conditions, the circuit of Fig. 2-11 will operate exactly as described previously, with the exception that only one half of the complete circuit will become active—that is, either the upper byte RAM will be enabled onto the system data bus, or the lower byte RAM will be enabled onto the system data bus. The byte that is not enabled onto the system data bus will remain in the tristate condition and will be floating electrically.

Let us now follow the logic of Fig. 2-11 for the operation of writing a word (16 bits) to the system RAM. The input lines of Fig. 2-11 will be as follows:

1. R/$\overline{\text{W}}$ will be a logical 0. This indicates a WRITE operation.
2. $\overline{\text{MSELA}}$ will be a logical 0. This is the active mode for the signal.

Under these conditions, input pin 5 of IC1 and IC2 in Fig. 2-11 will be a logical 0, enabling these OR gates. When the $\overline{\text{UDS}}$ and the $\overline{\text{LDS}}$ timed control signals from the 68000 are asserted, pin 11 of IC1 and IC2 will become a logical 0. This action forces output pin 6 of IC1 and IC2 to a logical 0. Output pin 6 of IC1 and IC2 is connected to the $\overline{\text{WE}}$ inputs to the 2114 RAMs.

After one gate delay, the $\overline{\text{CE}}$ input to the 2114 RAMs is set to a logical 0. This is due to output pins 3 and 6 of the 74LS08 AND gate being set to a logical 0 via input pins 2 and 5. This sequence of events is exactly what is required when data are written to the 2114 common I/O memory. (See Fig. 2-10.) That is, the $\overline{\text{WE}}$ input to the RAM becomes active before the memory chip is enabled via the $\overline{\text{CE}}$ input pin. This will prevent any bus conflict from occurring between the memory output lines and the bidirectional memory data buffer outputs.

It can be seen from the schematic of Fig. 2-11 that the bidirectional data buffers do not have the direction control line changed from a logical 1 to a logical 0 during a memory WRITE operation. When writing data to either the upper byte or the lower byte of memory, only the section of Fig. 2-11 that provides the control inputs to the memory will be active. The other byte does not have either the $\overline{\text{CS}}$ or the $\overline{\text{WE}}$ asserted.

2-6: A COMPLETE SCHEMATIC OF A 1K × 16-BIT RAM

Figure 2-12 shows the complete schematic for a 1K × 16-bit static RAM system that will communicate with a 68000. We have discussed all of the circuits shown in Fig. 2-12 on an individual basis. These circuits are now connected to form a complete, working 1K × 16-bit static RAM system.

Note that $\overline{\text{MSELB}}$ decoded memory line is not used in this example. The bidirectional data buffers are 74LS245's. These are the same buffers that were discussed in Chap. 1 for the bidirectional buffering of the microprocessor data lines.

Finally, the memory devices, the 2114's, are connected to the address bus, the data bus, and the memory control lines in the

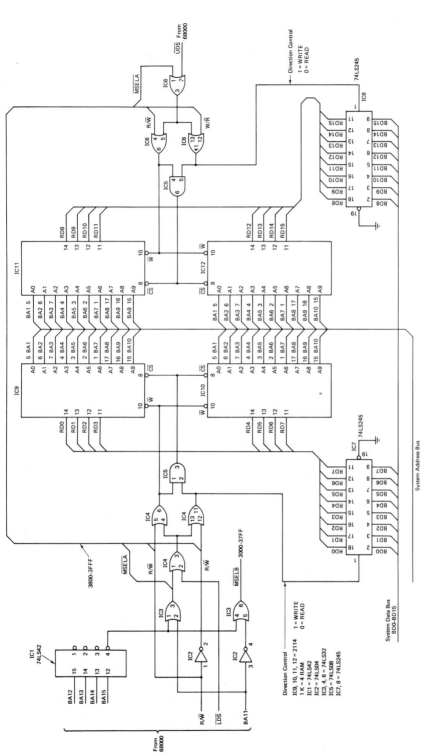

FIGURE 2–12. Schematic diagram of a complete schematic for a 1K × 16 static *RAM* for the 68000.

47

manner that was described previously. IC9 and IC10 are the lower data bytes D0–D7 of the memory. IC11 and IC12 are the upper data bytes D8–D15 of the memory.

2-7:   SEQUENCE OF EVENTS FOR A RAM READ

Let us now discuss the sequence of electrical events required for the 68000 to perform the function of a memory READ from the system RAM. As each step in the sequence is given, you are asked to refer to the schematic shown in Fig. 2-12. This diagram will help to verify the hardware response to each event. The electrical sequence is as follows:

1. A1–A23 are set to the memory address from which data are to be read. We are using address lines A1–A15 only in this example.
2. $\overline{AS}$ is set to a logical 0.

When this sequence occurs, the memory address is stable and applied to the system memory address inputs. The address decoders will generate the correct memory address space lines, $\overline{MSELA}$ or $\overline{MSELB}$. It should be pointed out that $\overline{AS}$ need not be electrically used by the system hardware. We list it in the sequence of events because this signal represents the point in time when the address is stable to the external hardware from the 68000.

3. R/$\overline{W}$ is set to a logical 1 for a READ operation.

These three events are under the control of the 68000. These outputs are set to the logical conditions dictated by the system software and will occur early in the memory operation cycle. The R/$\overline{W}$, $\overline{AS}$, and address lines may be thought of as static control events—that is, once set by the 68000 they will not change their logical state for the entire memory cycle.

4. The $\overline{UDS}$, $\overline{LDS}$, or both control lines are set to a logical 0. This action electrically informs the system hardware that the 68000 is prepared to receive data from the memory.

When these signals go to a logical 0, the data from the system memory are enabled onto the system data bus BD0–BD15 through the bidirectional data buffers IC7 and IC8 of Fig. 2-12.

5. Next, the external hardware must set the $\overline{\text{DTACK}}$ input to the 68000 to a logical 0. Our system will accomplish this exactly the same way as shown in Chap. 1. We will show other techniques for realizing this function later in this chapter.

6. $\overline{\text{UDS}}$, $\overline{\text{LDS}}$, or both control lines are set to a logical 1 by the 68000.

7. $\overline{\text{AS}}$ is set to a logical 1 by the 68000.

Events 6 and 7 terminate the overall system operation. The external hardware is electrically informed that the memory cycle is complete.

2-8: SEQUENCE OF EVENTS FOR A RAM WRITE

In this section, we will discuss the sequence of electrical events for writing data to the system RAM with the 68000. You may refer to Fig. 2-12 to verify the effect of each event on the system hardware. The sequence is as follows:

1. A1–A23 are set to the memory address where data will be written.

2. $\overline{\text{AS}}$ is set to a logical 0 under the control of the 68000.

The address decoders are now enabled to generate the correct address space enable lines, $\overline{\text{MSELA}}$ or $\overline{\text{MSELB}}$.

3. $\text{R}/\overline{\text{W}}$ is set to a logical 0, indicating a WRITE operation.

4. D0–D15 will place data to be written to the memory on the system data bus. The origin of data is from the 68000.

Referring to Fig. 2-12, we see that the data on the system data bus are placed directly at the 2114 data input pins. The bidirectional buffers are enabled in the correct direction. However, the 2114 device has not been electrically informed of a WRITE operation, nor has the 2114 been electrically selected.

5. $\overline{\text{UDS}}$, $\overline{\text{LDS}}$, or both are set to a logical 0 under the control of the 68000.

When these signals are set to a logical 0, the 2114 has the $\overline{\text{WE}}$ and the $\overline{\text{CS}}$ input lines asserted. This is accomplished by the control circuits that were discussed in Fig. 2-11. The data that are currently on the system data bus are now written into the system memory at the address specified by the system address address bus.

6. The system hardware now sets the $\overline{\text{DTACK}}$ input to the 68000 to a logical 0.
7. $\overline{\text{UDS}}$, $\overline{\text{LDS}}$, or both are set to a logical 1 by the 68000. On this edge of the $\overline{\text{UDS}}$ or $\overline{\text{LDS}}$ signals, the WRITE data should be strobed into the memory.
8. $\overline{\text{AS}}$ is set to a logical 1 under the control of the 68000.

THE HARDWARE OPERATION IS NOW COMPLETE.

2-9: SUMMARY OF READ AND WRITE EVENTS

The following is a list of the sequence of electrical events for reading and writing data to the system RAM. Refer to this list in later chapters, when we discuss troubleshooting the system.

READ Sequence

1. A1–A23 are set to the address for the memory read.
2. $\overline{\text{AS}}$ is set to a logical 0.
3. $\text{R}/\overline{\text{W}}$ is set to a logical 1.
4. $\overline{\text{UDS}}$, $\overline{\text{LDS}}$, or both are set to a logical 0.
5. $\overline{\text{DTACK}}$ is set to a logical 0 via external hardware.
6. $\overline{\text{UDS}}$ and $\overline{\text{LDS}}$ are set to a logical 1.
7. $\overline{\text{AS}}$ is set to a logical 1.

This terminates the system READ operation.

WRITE Sequence

1. A1–A23 are set to the address for the memory write.
2. $\overline{\text{AS}}$ is set to a logical 0.
3. $\text{R}/\overline{\text{W}}$ is set to a logical 0.
4. D0–D15 are set to the data to be written at the address specified.

5. $\overline{UDS}$, $\overline{LDS}$, or both are set to a logical 0.

6. $\overline{DTACK}$ is set to a logical 0 via external hardware.

7. $\overline{UDS}$ and $\overline{LDS}$ are set to a logical 1.

8. $\overline{AS}$ is set to a logical 1.

The memory WRITE operation is complete.

2-10: EXTENDING READ AND WRITE ACCESS TIME WITH $\overline{DTACK}$

In this section, we will discuss how the read and write access time for a memory operation can be extended using the $\overline{DTACK}$ input to the 68000. We will show a circuit that will allow a preset delay to occur. Further, the circuit will delay only during a particular address space—that is, one section of physical memory may be slower than another. When the slow memory space is enabled, the $\overline{DTACK}$ input will be delayed.

To begin this discussion, let us review the function of the $\overline{DTACK}$ input to the 68000. When the 68000 asserts the $\overline{UDS}$ or the $\overline{LDS}$ control signal, it electrically informs the external hardware that the CPU is ready to receive data for a READ operation or output data for a WRITE operation. The external hardware must now electrically inform the 68000 if it is electrically prepared to receive or send data.

There are several reasons for the external hardware not being prepared:

1. The memory has not had enough time to access the address location.

2. The dynamic RAM is being refreshed.

3. The external device is waiting for some other hardware response before sending or receiving data from the 68000.

Whatever the reason, we will assume that the external hardware is not electrically prepared to complete the communication started by the 68000.

To solve this problem, we will delay the $\overline{DTACK}$ input to the 68000 for an integer number of clock cycles. This is equivalent to delaying the $\overline{DTACK}$ for a certain amount of time. Further, we can set the amount of time to be delayed via a DIP switch. Figure 2-13 shows a schematic of this type of circuit.

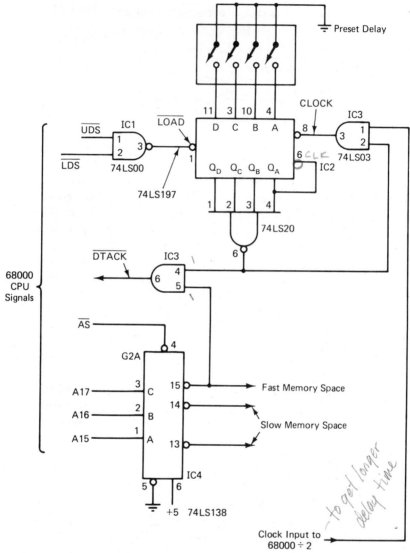

FIGURE 2–13. Schematic diagram for generating delays using the $\overline{DTACK}$ input signal to the 68000.

The circuit of Fig. 2-13 operates in this way: We must first assume that the 68000 is starting a new memory READ or WRITE cycle and that the $\overline{UDS}$, $\overline{LDS}$, and $\overline{AS}$ control lines are a logical 1. With $\overline{AS}$ at the logical 1 level, the output pins 13, 14, and 15 of IC4 are a logical 1. Pin 3 of the 74LS00 NAND gate, IC1, is a logical 0 due to $\overline{UDS}$ and $\overline{LDS}$ at a logical 1.

When pin 3 of IC1 is a logical 0, the load input to the 74LS197 counter, IC2, is a logical 0. A logical 0 on the load input will preset the QA, QB, QC, QD outputs of the counter. The Q outputs will be preset to the logical value set on the A, B, C, D inputs. These inputs are connected to a DIP switch. When the switch is closed, the input is a logical 0. When the switch is open, the input is a logical 1.

Let us now assume that input switches A and B are closed. This means that the logical state of the inputs to the counter are 1 1 0 0. This is "C" in hexadecimal notation. With the $\overline{\text{UDS}}$ and $\overline{\text{LDS}}$ outputs from the 68000 in the logical 1 state, the outputs of the counter are preset to 1 1 0 0. With the load input to the counter in the logical 0 state, the clock inputs to the counter will have no effect.

Next, let us assume that the $\overline{\text{AS}}$ output from the 68000 has been set to a logical 0. The 74LS138 device will now become enabled. If the address space was decoded as "fast memory space," the input to the AND gate, IC3, pin 5, will be a logical 0. The $\overline{\text{DTACK}}$ input to the 68000 will then be a logical 0. The result will be no delay. The logical state of the counter is of no consequence for the "fast memory space."

Assume now that the system address space is decoding the "slow memory space." In this instance, output pin 15 of the 74LS138 will be a logical 1. The input to the AND gate, IC3, pin 5, will be a logical 1. $\overline{\text{DTACK}}$ is not asserted. The output of the 74LS20 NAND gate, pin 6, is now dependent on the counter action.

The 68000 now asserts the $\overline{\text{UDS}}$, $\overline{\text{LDS}}$, or both control signals, and the $\overline{\text{DTACK}}$ input to the 68000 is a logical 1 due to both input pins 4 and 5 of the AND gate IC3 being a logical 1. When either $\overline{\text{UDS}}$ or $\overline{\text{LDS}}$ becomes asserted, the load input to the 74LS197 counter is set to a logical 1. The counter will begin to count at the input clock rate.

The count starts at the "preset" value of 1 1 0 0. Count advances by one at each clock input. The count sequence is 1 1 0 1, 1 1 1 0, 1 1 1 1. When the count reaches 1 1 1 1, the four inputs to the 74LS20 NAND gate are all logical 1. The output of the NAND gate will be a logical 0. This logical 0 will force the output of the 74LS08 pin 6 to a logical 0. The $\overline{\text{DTACK}}$ input to the 68000 is now set to a logical 0. This action will end the delay, and the 68000 will resume normal execution of the READ or WRITE cycle.

When output pin 6 of the 74LS20 becomes a logical 0, the clock input to the counter is halted. At the end of the 68000 memory cycle, the $\overline{\text{UDS}}$, $\overline{\text{LDS}}$, and $\overline{\text{AS}}$ control lines are again set to a logical 1. The sequence of events now starts over with the load input to the counter becoming a logical 0.

From this discussion, it can be seen that up to 15 clock cycles of the 74LS197 can be delayed. Note that the clock input frequency is one-half of the 68000 clock frequency. This will give a total delay of thirty (30) 68000 clock cycles. The total delay can be determined by setting the switches on the counter preset inputs. A technique such as this will allow a system to perform at maximum speed, based on the type or grade of memories. If the grade of memories has a fast access time, then the delay can be eliminated by setting all of the switches to open. This will preset the counter to 1 1 1 1. If the memories are such that the access time is slower, the system can still operate but at a reduced speed. Figures 2-14 and 2-15 show important signal relationships for the schematic of Fig. 2-13.

It must be stressed that the technique shown here is an example of how the $\overline{\text{DTACK}}$ input to the 68000 can be used to delay the communication process. Several points were brought out in the discussion that may be of help when designing or troubleshooting different systems.

2-11:   CHAPTER SUMMARY

In this chapter, the details of how the 68000 communicates with static RAM were discussed using the 2114 common I/O RAM as the main memory. This RAM was chosen because it is in wide general use in the industry. Further, if one can understand the details for using this memory, then relating these details to other memories will be an easier task.

The circuits shown in this chapter were designed to demonstrate what is needed to perform electrical communication between the 68000 and a static RAM.

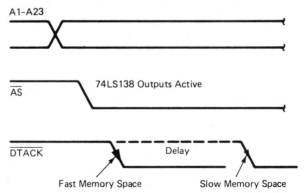

FIGURE 2–14.   Timing diagram showing how the $\overline{\text{DTACK}}$ input to the 68000 will be delayed for slow memories.

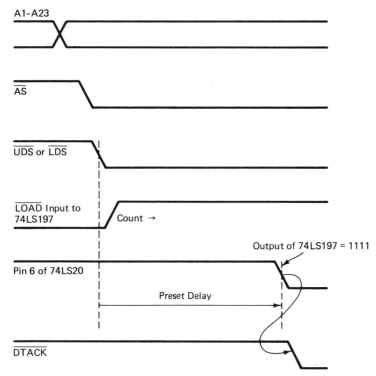

FIGURE 2–15. Timing diagram showing relationships of different signals of Fig. 2–13.

There are many different techniques that can be employed to realize each of the circuits described in this chapter. It was felt that if the reader could actually see how it could be accomplished, and follow the logic all the way, then improving on the scheme would be natural for the user and system designer. For the hardware person who will be troubleshooting the system, knowing how the system is supposed to operate is the first step. Once it is understood how the 68000 performs the communication, then following the logic of a particular system as it realizes this function is made easier.

The sequence of events that the 68000 will perform whenever a static RAM operation occurs in the system was presented. This sequence is a very valuable tool for the system troubleshooter. Using this sequence of events and Static Stimulus Testing, a quick verification of the hardware of the system can be made. A clear demonstration of how this works will be given later in the text in a troubleshooting problem.

Finally, we presented a technique for extending the READ or WRITE access time. This technique employed the use of delaying the $\overline{\text{DTACK}}$ input to the 68000.

CHAPTER 3

68000 INPUT AND OUTPUT (I/O)

Two major hardware operations that a microprocessor performs electrically are reading data from an input device and writing data to an output device. To troubleshoot and interface microprocessor hardware effectively, a firm understanding of these hardware operations is required. This chapter will focus on the details of how the 68000 performs electrical communication with an input and output device.

A general input and output (I/O) port will be designed. The port will be constructed using discrete logic devices. We present I/O at this point because electrical communication with I/O is similar to operations performed with static RAM. In fact, as we progress through this chapter, you will be able to see strong similarities in communications between the microprocessor and static RAM and to and from the microprocessor and I/O. The 68000 is designed for use with a memory-mapped I/O architecture. Therefore, the software of the 68000 makes no distinction between memory and I/O communications. The difference is in the external circuits that comprise the input and output ports.

3-1: OVERVIEW OF 68000 I/O

There are three major types of hardware I/O operations that are performed by the 68000 (see Fig. 3-1). No matter what software instruction may be used to generate the I/O operation, the hardware will electrically respond in the manner described in this chapter. In Fig. 3-1, we can see that the microprocessor will electrically read or write an entire word (16 bits) in a parallel fashion to or from an I/O device, or it will electrically read or write a byte (8 bits) to or from an I/O device.

In the byte mode, the 68000 will read or write from the upper byte (D8–D15) or the lower byte (D0–D7). These electrical actions are very similar to reading or writing data to static RAM. It should

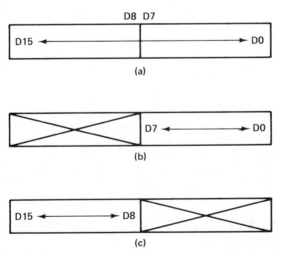

FIGURE 3–1. Block diagram showing the possible communication between the 68000 and an input or output port.
a) The 68000 can read or write an entire word (16 bits) during a single I/O transfer.
b) The 68000 can read or write data to bits D0–D7 only. The "X" indicates the upper byte of the data will not be disturbed during this particular I/O transfer.
c) The 68000 can read or write data to bits D8–D15 only. The "X" indicates the lower byte of the data will not be disturbed during this particular I/O transfer.

be mentioned that I/O operations on 1 byte only, 8 bits, make the 68000 compatible with many standard I/O devices used with 8-bit microprocessors. We will discuss how to interface to 6800 I/O devices and concentrate on the interface of a 6800 PIA in Chap. 4.

3-2: THE PORT ADDRESS

As stated previously, the 68000 supports only one type of I/O architecture, memory-mapped I/O. In a 68000 system, all 23 address lines are available for I/O decoding. If your background in 8-bit microprocessors includes 6800 experience, then this is not a new concept for you. Some of the 8-bit microprocessors, such as the 8080 and the 8085, use only 8 of the total 16 address lines to address I/O ports. If memory-mapped, linear select I/O is used, there are now 22 unique I/O ports. This is more than twice the number available using linear select I/O in most 8-bit microprocessors.

The address lines used for I/O addressing are the same as those used for system memory addressing. It will be shown later how the microprocessor will electrically separate the memory requests from the I/O requests. Not all 23 address lines need be used for system I/O, just as we do not need to use all available address lines for system memory. The general I/O port we will consider in this chapter will use all 23 address lines.

Each I/O port in a system will respond to a unique combination of bits on the address bus. The address combination is called the "port address." Port addresses for the I/O device under consideration are designated FFFFFE or FFFFFF. The port will electrically respond to either of these system address combinations. Figure 3-2 shows a schematic diagram for detecting this port address. Notice that we show only 22 address lines in the I/O address of Fig. 3-2. Address line A23 will be used to separate the I/O space from the memory space. When A23 is a logical 1, I/O is wanted. When A23 is a logical 0, memory is wanted.

Referring to Fig. 3-2, we see that output pin 8 of all 74LS30's will be logical 0 if, and only if, all input lines are logical 1. The output of the 74LS32 OR gate (pin 3) will be a logical 0 only when both NAND gate outputs, IC1 and IC2, are a logical 0. Output pin 3 of the 74LS32 is connected to input pin 4. When both input pins 4 and 5 of the 74LS32 OR gate are a logical 0, output pin 6 is a logical 0. Output pin 6 is labeled the "port select" line. The port select line is only active logical 0 when the system address bus is logically equal to the unique select code of the port.

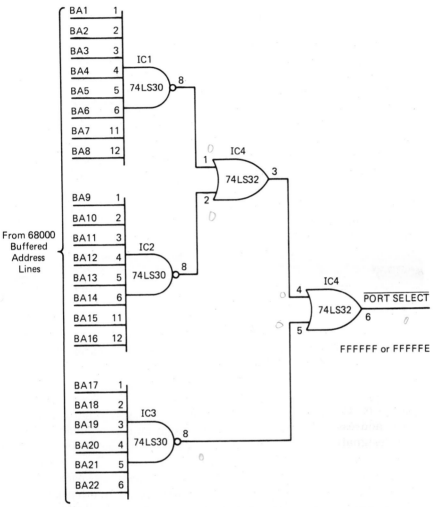

FIGURE 3–2. Schematic diagram showing how the port select signal can be generated with hardware. The port will respond to address *FFFFFF* or *FFFFFE.*

Note that the port select line can become active even when no I/O communication is occurring in the system. This is due to the fact that the system memory is also using the same address lines. For example, if the microprocessor is reading data from the memory address 7FFFFE or 7FFFFF, the port select line of Fig. 3-2 will become active. This fact is important to know for the hardware troubleshooter. When checking a microprocessor controlled system, do not be surprised if the port select line gives indications of being selected even at a time when no software instructions indicate system communication with the port. This is a valid condition and should not lead you to think there is a malfunction.

3-3: GENERATING THE $\overline{\text{IORQ}}$ CONTROL LINE

In this section, we will discuss how the 68000 can be made to generate the electrical signal which indicates that an I/O operation will occur. The 68000 is unlike the 8086 and the Z8000 16-bit microprocessors in that those two microprocessors support a separate I/O architecture. Only one I/O architecture is supported by the 68000. This is the *memory-mapped I/O architecture*.

Memory-mapped I/O architecture means that some of the system memory space is reserved solely for input and output operations. The advantage of this type of I/O architecture is that all memory software operations are available for use with I/O. A disadvantage of memory-mapped I/O is that a portion of the available memory space is used up.

Regardless of the advantages or disadvantages of memory-mapped I/O, it is the only choice to be made when using the 68000. With this fact in mind, an electrical output signal must be generated that is under the control of the 68000. The 68000 will indicate that an I/O operation is about to occur in the system hardware.

The technique we will use is quite simple—i.e., address line A23. Whenever address line A23 is a logical 1, the 68000 will be performing I/O. This technique is also quite wasteful in terms of memory space. In fact, one-half of the system memory space is used for I/O. In some systems, this may be satisfactory. In other applications, a portion of the system address bus can be decoded to generate the $\overline{\text{IORQ}}$ control line.

In the examples that follow, the use of address line A23 to generate the $\overline{\text{IORQ}}$ line will be shown.

3-4: GENERATION OF THE PORT WRITE SIGNAL

The port write signal for a 68000 system will be defined as the write enable strobe for a unique output port. The port write must be qualified by both the $\overline{\text{PORT SELECT}}$ and the $\overline{\text{IORQ}}$ signal. The function of the port write signal is to provide the active digital signal by which the data from the microprocessor is latched or written into an output port.

With the output port data width defined as 16 bits, the 68000 has the capability of communicating electrically with the upper byte, lower byte, or the entire 16-bit word. The hardware must provide a write strobe that is active on the upper byte, lower byte, or both bytes. We must keep this goal in mind when the hardware is designed in order to achieve this capability. The diagram of Fig. 3-3 shows the general timing sequence that will be used. Notice in that illustration that all of the control signals, except $\overline{UDS}$ and $\overline{LDS}$, can be thought of as static control logic levels. These signals voltage levels will remain stable for the entire hardware operation. Using this concept and the timing diagram of Fig. 3-3, the schematic of Fig. 3-4 can be realized.

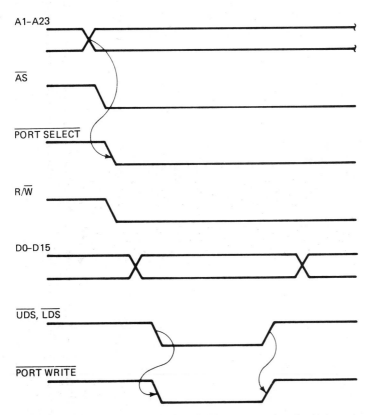

FIGURE 3-3. Timing diagram of the important signals during an output *WRITE* operation with the 68000.

Referring to Fig. 3-4, the inputs to OR gate pins 1 and 2 are PORT SELECT and A23. During an output operation, A23 will be a logical 1 and the PORT SELECT will be a logical 0. Further, if the 68000 is performing an output WRITE operation, the R/W line will be a logical 0.

With the input lines of Fig. 3-4 set to the logical conditions just described, output pin 3 of IC1 will be a logical 0 and output pin 6 of IC1 will be a logical 0. With output pin 6 a logical 0, the two OR gates with output pins 11 and 8 will be enabled.

With these two OR gates becoming enabled, either the upper byte of data, the lower byte of data, or both bytes will be strobed. When the UDS, LDS, or both of these timed control signals are asserted by the 68000, output pin 11, output pin 8, or both outputs will be asserted.

Using the logic of Fig. 3-4, the upper or lower output port byte strobe can be enabled. It would be an electrical communication disaster to assert both the upper and lower byte strobes during a byte operation in that the byte which was supposed to be left undisturbed would be changed as well as the byte that was meant to be changed.

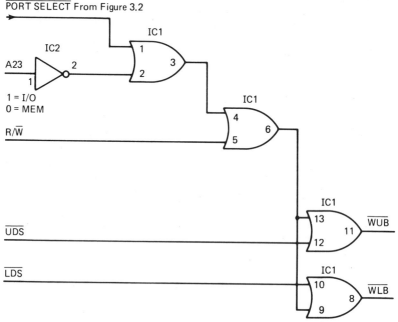

FIGURE 3–4. Schematic diagram showing how the port write strobes will be generated with hardware.

Note, however, that it would be a problem only if both upper and lower bytes of the selected I/O port were being used. An 8-bit I/O port can be designed and used with the 68000. The data inputs to the port are connected, to either the upper bits D8–D15 or the lower bits D0–D7. The port write is then designed to operate on either the upper or the lower byte.

3-5: GENERATION OF THE PORT READ SIGNAL

The discussion will now center on how the 68000 performs the function of reading data from a 16-bit input port. In this discussion, it should be noted that the microprocessor can perform input operations on either the upper byte or the lower byte. However, when reading data, there need not be as much concern with this fact as with writing data to an output port. This is because the hardware

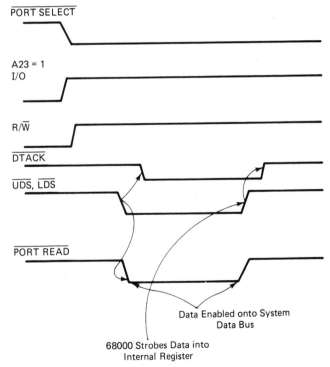

FIGURE 3–5. Timing diagram of the important signals during an input *READ* operation with the 68000.

can enable both bytes on the system data bus and let the 68000 electrically input the byte it requires. This is feasible only if the bidirectional buffers on the 68000 cause no bus conflicts on either the upper or the lower byte. If no bidirectional buffers are used, this need not be of concern. This same reasoning was used in Chap. 1, where the 68000 was reading data from system ROM. Keeping this in mind, let us examine the important points of an input operation.

The timing diagram of Fig. 3-5 gives a general sequence of electrical events that will occur during an input port read operation. The port select signal is exactly the same as was shown for the output port select signal. The $\overline{\text{IORQ}}$ signal is the same as was generated for an output operation. The R/$\overline{\text{W}}$ signal will be a logical 1, indicative of a READ operation.

Two important signals shown in Fig. 3-5 are the $\overline{\text{UDS}}$ and $\overline{\text{LDS}}$ timed control lines. These are timed signals sent to the input port hardware that will electrically start the data transfer. When one or both of these signals goes to a logical 0, the data from the input port are placed onto the system data bus. During that time, the input port data are input to the physical data pins of the 68000. Later, $\overline{\text{UDS}}$ and $\overline{\text{LDS}}$ will go to a logical 1. When this occurs, the input port

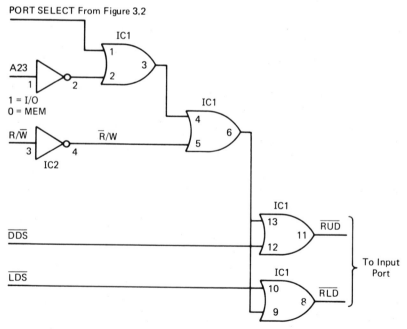

FIGURE 3–6. Schematic diagram showing how the port read strobes will be generated with hardware.

data are latched into the 68000 CPU and electrically removed from the system data bus.

Figure 3-6 shows one way to generate a port read signal based on the logical conditions of the timing diagram shown in Fig. 3-5. In Fig. 3-6, the output pin 3 of IC1 will be a logical 0 if, and only if, the $\overline{\text{PORT SELECT}}$ is a logical 0 and A23 is a logical 1. This is the active state of an enabled input port. Pin 3 of the 74LS32, IC1, is input to pin 4 of IC1. Pin 5 is the inverted logical condition of the $\overline{\text{R/W}}$ control signal from the 68000. When the $\overline{\text{R/W}}$ is a logical 1, indicating a READ operation, pin 5 of the 74LS32, IC1, is a logical 0. With both pins 4 and 5 a logical 0, output pin 6 will be a logical 0.

A logical 0 on pin 6 will set pins 13 and 9 of the 74LS32, IC1, to a logical 0. When $\overline{\text{UDS}}$, $\overline{\text{LDS}}$, or both timed control signals from the 68000 are a logical 0, output pin 11, 8, or both will become a logical 0. These output pins are used by the system input port to place the data electrically from the input port onto the system data bus. In effect, these signals will be the tri-state control signal for the input port.

3-6:   COMPLETE SCHEMATIC FOR AN I/O PORT

In this section, the sequence of events for an I/O READ and WRITE operation will be presented. As the sequence is given, reference will be made to Fig. 3-7, which shows the complete schematic for a general 16-bit I/O port. At each particular step in the sequence, a discussion of the corresponding hardware response that occurs will be given. We start with the 68000 performing an output operation.

1. First, address lines A1–A23 are set to the desired output address under the control of the 68000.

The output address lines are now decoded by the port select hardware that was shown in Fig. 3-1. In Fig. 3-7, we see that input pin 4 of IC3 will become active logical 0 when the correct system address is output.

2. The $\overline{\text{AS}}$ signal now goes to a logical 0 under the control of the 68000.

This signal indicates that the address lines contain a stable address. $\overline{\text{AS}}$ will remain a logical 0 until the end of the current memory cycle. The $\overline{\text{AS}}$ signal does not have to be used in applying the address to the system.

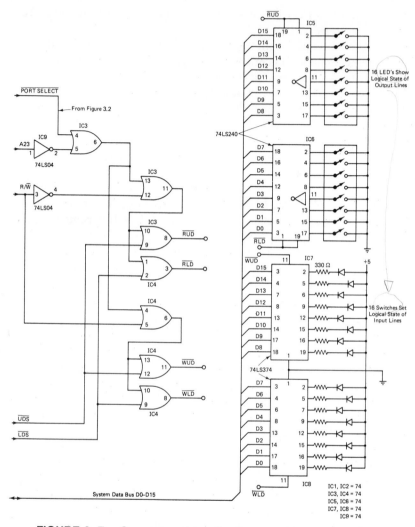

FIGURE 3–7. Complete schematic diagram of a general 16-bit input and output port for use with the 68000. The port will respond to I/O address *FFFFFF* or *FFFFFE*.

3. Next, the R/W̄ is set to a logical 0, indicative of a WRITE operation.

4. The 68000 now outputs the electrical data to be written to the output port. In Fig. 3-7, notice that data inputs are now valid at the 74LS374 octal latches, IC7 and IC8.

5. UDS, LDS, or both are set to a logical 0 by the 68000.

These signals will clock the inputs to either one (byte) or both (word) of the 74LS374 latches IC7 and IC9 to a logical 0. The 74LS374 will strobe the data into the latch on the positive-going edge of the clock signal.

6. Next, the $\overline{\text{DTACK}}$ is asserted by the external hardware. This action will occur in the same way as described for a memory operation.

7. $\overline{\text{UDS}}$, $\overline{\text{LDS}}$, and $\overline{\text{AS}}$ are set to a logical 1 by the 68000.

When this occurs, the clock inputs to the 74LS374 latches are set to a logical 1. The data that was present at the latch inputs is strobed into the device. The positive-going edge of this signal is the end of the I/O WRITE operation. The microprocessor sets up to perform another hardware operation electrically.

Let us now discuss the sequence of events that the 68000 will perform when reading data from the input port of Fig. 3-7. The major events that will occur in an I/O READ operation are the same as for an I/O WRITE operation except that the R/$\overline{\text{W}}$ control signal is a logical 1. This indicates a READ operation.

The 74LS32 OR gate, IC4 of Fig. 3-7, will have input pin 5 at a logical 1. This is due to the R/$\overline{\text{W}}$ input pin 3 of IC9 at a logical 1 state. With this input in the logical 1 state, the port write strobes will be disabled. In this fashion, the output operation is electrically disabled when performing an input read.

At this time, the input port decoding logic IC3, IC4, will have a logical 0 on pins 10 and 1. The data from the input port is not yet enabled onto the system data bus. The hardware is waiting for the timed control signal $\overline{\text{UDS}}$ or $\overline{\text{LDS}}$ to become active.

$\overline{\text{UDS}}$ OR $\overline{\text{LDS}}$ ARE SET TO A LOGICAL 0 BY THE 68000.

This is a hardware indication that the microprocessor is electrically ready to receive data from the input port. When $\overline{\text{UDS}}$ or $\overline{\text{LDS}}$ is a logical 0, the enable input lines pins 1 and 19 of the 74LS240's IC5 and IC6 are set to a logical 0. This logical condition will enable these devices. The result is that whatever data was at the input to the 74LS240 buffers is now output to the system data bus. During this time, the data will be logically placed on the 68000 data input lines.

$\overline{\text{DTACK}}$ INPUT IS SET TO A LOGICAL 0 VIA THE EXTERNAL HARDWARE.

$$\overline{\text{UDS}}, \overline{\text{LDS}}, \text{AND } \overline{\text{AS}} \text{ ARE SET TO A LOGICAL 1 BY THE}$$
$$68000.$$

At this time, the data from the input port are strobed into the 68000 and are removed electrically from the system data bus. The system operation is now complete.

3-7: SUMMARY OF ELECTRICAL EVENTS FOR AN I/O OPERATION

In this section, a list of electrical sequences of events that will occur for an input and output operation with the 68000 is given.

Output WRITE Sequence

1. A1–A23 are set to the correct output port address.
2. $\overline{\text{AS}}$ is set to a logical 0.
3. R/$\overline{\text{W}}$ is set to a logical 0.
4. D0–D15 are set to the correct data to be written to the output port.
5. $\overline{\text{UDS}}$, $\overline{\text{LDS}}$, or both are set to a logical 0.
6. $\overline{\text{DTACK}}$ is set to a logical 0 via external hardware.
7. $\overline{\text{UDS}}$, $\overline{\text{LDS}}$, and $\overline{\text{AS}}$ are set to a logical 1.

Input READ Sequence

1. A1–A23 are set to the correct input port address.
2. $\overline{\text{AS}}$ is set to a logical 0.
3. R/$\overline{\text{W}}$ is set to a logical 1.
4. $\overline{\text{UDS}}$, $\overline{\text{LDS}}$, or both are set to a logical 0.
5. $\overline{\text{DTACK}}$ input is set to a logical 0 via external hardware.
6. $\overline{\text{UDS}}$, $\overline{\text{LDS}}$, and $\overline{\text{AS}}$ are set to a logical 1.

3-8: $\overline{\text{DTACK}}$ INPUT FOR AN I/O OPERATION

When the 68000 performs a standard I/O operation, the $\overline{\text{DTACK}}$ input to the device must be asserted by external hardware. This is exactly what was done for a memory operation. We will assume in this input and output operation that the I/O device is fast enough to respond to the 68000 with no additional wait states. Therefore we will assert the $\overline{\text{DTACK}}$ input to the 68000 exactly the same as for static RAM. This technique was shown in detail in Chap. 1. The circuit is repeated here in Fig. 3-8.

3-9: CHAPTER SUMMARY

In this chapter, we have presented and discussed how the 68000 performs general input and output operations. Some hardware decoding techniques were shown and discussed. The designs given in this chapter are meant only as instructional aids. At the end of this chapter, the complete sequence of events that will occur during an input and output operation were listed.

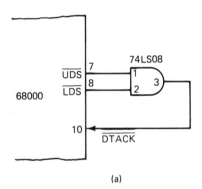

(a)

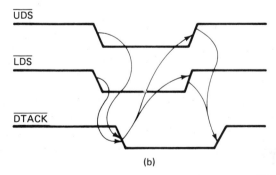

(b)

FIGURE 3–8a. Schematic diagram showing how the $\overline{\text{DTACK}}$ input to the 68000 will be asserted in the I/O cycle.
FIGURE 3–8b. Timing diagram showing the timing relationship between the $\overline{\text{UDS}}$, $\overline{\text{LDS}}$ and $\overline{\text{DTACK}}$ signals for the 68000.

For the person who will troubleshoot or debug the hardware of a 68000 system, learning this sequence of events is a good starting point to understanding the hardware of I/O operations. Reference will be made to this sequence of events in later chapters, where the details of troubleshooting an input and output port using Static Stimulus Testing are covered.

CHAPTER 4

INTERFACING A 68000 TO A 6800 PERIPHERAL DEVICE

In this chapter, we will discuss how to interface a 6800 peripheral device to a 68000 microprocessor. The I/O device we will use is the Motorola 6821 PIA. PIA stands for "Peripheral Interface Adapter." It will be shown how the I/O device is enabled and communicated with in a system environment. The discussion will be general enough so that you may see how these types of devices are used with the 68000. However, we will also be specific so that you may see exactly how to interface this particular device.

The discussion will start with a review of the PIA device, and we will not go into great detail concerning device operation. Such a discussion is better suited to a manufacturer's data sheet. Rather, the PIA will be presented at a level of discussion that will allow you to understand how it can communicate with the 68000 microprocessor.

Following the review of the PIA, we will show how the device operates in a typical system. The discussion of a particular PIA will allow you to see exactly how the 68000 can electrically communicate with what is basically an 8-bit I/O device.

Finally, after explaining how the PIA operates in the system environment, we will show some 68000 software that will allow electrical communication between the 6821 PIA and the CPU.

4-1: OVERVIEW OF THE MOTOROLA 6821 PIA

In this section, we will discuss how the 6821 PIA operates. The discussion will be limited to using the PIA in only two ways—that is, as a general 8-bit input port, or an 8-bit output port. The device is capable of many different operating modes. However, if we were to discuss each operating mode, it would require a chapter just on the device.

This discussion treats the PIA in an elementary form so that we may focus our efforts on how to interface the 68000 to the input and output device, rather than on how any specific device operates.

It is essential to know how the 6821 PIA operates in any specific system environment before making an attempt to interface or troubleshoot the circuit. We must know "what should be there"; otherwise measurements made and data acquired tell us nothing.

The 6821 PIA is shown in block diagram form in Fig. 4-1. We see in Fig. 4-1 that the device has three major groupings of I/O lines. These are Group A (PA), Group B (PB), and Control Group (CA, CB). The actual function of these lines is dependent on how the device is meant to be used in the system.

For example, Group A can be set to all output lines, and Group B can be set to all input lines. Both groups can be outputs or inputs. One should refer to the manufacturer's data sheet on this device for specific information on all of the modes of operation. A data sheet for the 6821 is given in the Appendix.

The mode we will be interested in is when groups A and B are outputs or inputs. To set the PIA in the mode we desire, it must be programmed. By "programmed," we mean the device must have

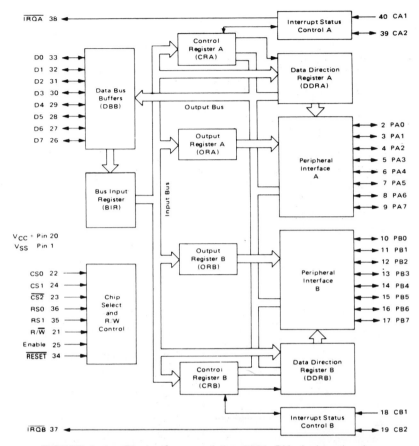

FIGURE 4–1. Block diagram of the 6821 *PIA* device showing basic internal registers.

data sent to it by the microprocessor. This data will define exactly how the groups at the output will behave electrically.

When the microprocessor is programming or "setting up" the PIA, data is sent to the device in exactly the same way as when the microprocessor is performing any output operation. The hardware of the system must inform the PIA electrically that the data being sent by the microprocessor is programming data and not output data. This is accomplished by asserting various logical inputs of the PIA. Let us discuss some of these inputs and what their function is in the device.

Figure 4-2 shows the physical input pins of the PIA. We see in Fig. 4-2 pins labeled "D0–D7." These are the data input and output

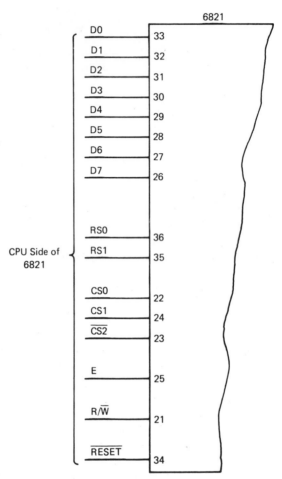

FIGURE 4–2. Pinout diagram for the *PIA* showing the inputs to the device from the microprocessor system.

lines for communication with the microprocessor. The PIA is an 8-bit device which requires only 8 data lines. This will not present a problem with the 16-bit 68000, as we will connect the 8 data lines to the upper or lower byte of a 16-bit data bus.

The next input pins on the PIA shown in Fig. 4-2 are labeled "CS0, CS1, and $\overline{CS2}$." These are the chip enable inputs. When CS0 = 1, CS1 = 1, and $\overline{CS2}$ = 0, the PIA device is enabled. With the device enabled, it is possible to establish electrical communication between the PIA and the microprocessor. The term "is possible" was used because other PIA input lines must be in the correct logical state to qualify the chip enable inputs to the device. The CS0, CS1, and $\overline{CS2}$ input pins perform a function similar to the chip enable input on the 2716 EPROMs that were discussed in Chap. 1.

The R/$\overline{W}$ input pin 21 on the PIA shown in Fig. 4-2 is active logical 1 whenever the microprocessor is reading data from the device. When this pin is a logical 0, the microprocessor is writing data to the device. Therefore, when the CS0, CS1, and $\overline{CS2}$ are all asserted, and the R/$\overline{W}$ is a logical 1, the microprocessor is reading data from the PIA. If the preceding conditions exist but the R/$\overline{W}$ line is a logical 0, the microprocessor is writing data to the PIA.

More control inputs labeled "RS0, RS1" are pins 35 and 36 shown in Fig. 4-2. These input signals define which internal group of registers the microprocessor is reading or writing data to during the I/O operation. Additional information on these input lines will be given when programming of the PIA is discussed.

Input pin 34 of Fig. 4-2 is labeled "RESET." This input line is normally connected to the system reset signal. By asserting this input, the PIA can be preset to a known operating state. This is useful so that no bus conflicts will exist at power up.

The final signal to discuss in Fig. 4-2 is the ENABLE (E) or clock input line. The clock is used to synchronize all transfers between the microprocessor and the PIA. Although the clock can be free-running, the PIA is not a dynamic device—that is, the clock can stop and no internal information will be lost. This fact will be useful when debugging the PIA using SST.

4-2: PROGRAMMING THE PIA

Now that we have had a brief introduction to the physical signals of the PIA, we will discuss how to use the device. First, we will set the PIA into a mode where it consists of two general-purpose 8-bit output ports—that is, a mode in which both port A and port B are functioning as output ports. This will give the device a total of 16 unique output lines. (See Fig. 4-3.)

To set up the PIA programming electrically, data must be written to it by the microprocessor. The programming data will define the function of ports A and B. The programming data that the microprocessor must write to the PIA is shown in Fig. 4-4. The correct data bytes were obtained from a data sheet on the PIA. One is asked to accept that these words will set up the PIA in the correct way.

The microprocessor will perform six output operations to the PIA. The first three bytes output will define the Group A I/O sig-

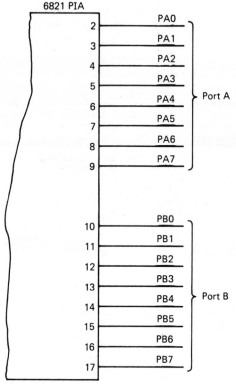

FIGURE 4–3. Pinout diagram of the device I/O lines showing both ports A and B programmed as outputs. This will result in a total of 16 physical output lines.

Function	RS1	RS0	DATA	
CONTROL REG A	0	1	00	
CONTROL REG B	1	1	00	
DATA REG A	0	0	FF	Set lines to Output
DATA REG B	1	0	FF	
CONTROL REG A	0	1	04	
CONTEOL REG B	1	1	04	
PA and PB = Output Ports				
WRITE DATA PA	0	0		
WRITE DATA PB	1	0		

FIGURE 4–4. *PIA* command words that will cause the 6821 to be programmed with both port A and port B as output ports.

nals. These signals will be defined as output only. This means that the entire group of lines labeled "PA0–PA7" are output lines from the PIA. To write data from the microprocessor into the internal registers of the PIA, certain external signals on the PIA must be in the proper logical state.

Signals under consideration are: CS0, CS1, $\overline{CS2}$, R/$\overline{W}$, RS0, RS1 and ENABLE (E). To program the Group A lines on the PIA, RS0, RS1 signal inputs will be (0 1), respectively. (See Fig. 4.4.) We are writing data into Control Register A. When writing data to the PIA, the device must be enabled. Therefore, the CS0, CS1, and $\overline{CS2}$ must be in the correct logical state for assertion.

If the PIA were interfaced to a 6800 microprocessor, one of the CS0 or CS1 lines would be connected to the $\overline{VMA}$ output line from the CPU. The other chip select lines will be decoded in a standard memory-mapped fashion.

The R/$\overline{W}$ input to the 6821 will be a logical 0, defining the I/O transfer as a WRITE operation. CPU data lines will output information to the 6821 data lines. The byte to be output will be 00 in hexadecimal.

Finally, the ENABLE input, which is usually Phase 2 for a 6800 system, will synchronize the transfer. (This is shown in the timing diagrams of Fig. 4-5.)

To program the Group A signals fully, the 6800 would write the data words to the internal registers as follows:

REGISTER	RS1	RS0	DATA (hexadecimal)
Control Register A	0	1	0 0
Data Register A	0	0	F F
Control Register A	0	1	0 4

The Group A signals are now ready to accept output data from the 6800 microprocessor and place the data on the port A lines as shown in Fig. 4-3.

The Group A signals are now programmed as outputs. The Group B signals have not been programmed. The data bytes to program the B group in the PIA are exactly the same as the bytes required to program the A group. The only difference in the programming is the inputs RS0 and RS1 must be set to different internal register numbers. This will indicate to the PIA that the registers for port B will be communicated with. The data words for programming port B to all outputs are as follows:

REGISTER	RS1	RS0	DATA (hexadecimal)
Control Register B	1	1	0 0
Data Register B	1	0	F F
Control Register B	1	1	0 4

Group B signals are now set up to output data from the 6800 microprocessor to the port B device pins, as shown in Fig. 4-3.

BUS TIMING CHARACTERISTICS (See Notes 1 and 2)

Ident. Number	Characteristic	Symbol	MC6821 Min	MC6821 Max	MC68A21 Min	MC68A21 Max	MC68B21 Min	MC68B21 Max	Unit
1	Cycle Time	t_{cyc}	1.0	10	0.67	10	0.5	10	µs
2	Pulse Width, E Low	PW_{EL}	430	–	280	–	210	–	ns
3	Pulse Width, E High	PW_{EH}	450	–	280	–	220	–	ns
4	Clock Rise and Fall Time	t_r, t_f	–	25	–	25	–	20	ns
9	Address Hold Time	t_{AH}	10	–	10	–	10	–	ns
13	Address Setup Time Before E	t_{AS}	80	–	60	–	40	–	ns
14	Chip Select Setup Time Before E	t_{CS}	80	–	60	–	40	–	ns
15	Chip Select Hold Time	t_{CH}	10	–	10	–	10	–	ns
18	Read Data Hold Time	t_{DHR}	20	100	20	100	20	100	ns
21	Write Data Hold Time	t_{DHW}	10	–	10	–	10	–	ms
30	Output Data Delay Time	t_{DDR}	–	290	–	180	–	150	ns
31	Input Data Setup Time	t_{DSW}	165	–	80	–	60	–	ns

FIGURE 1 — BUS TIMING

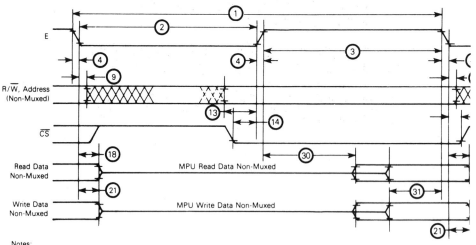

Notes:
1. Voltage levels shown are $V_L \leq 0.4$ V, $V_H \geq 2.4$ V, unless otherwise specified.
2. Measurement points shown are 0.8 V and 2.0 V, unless otherwise specified.

FIGURE 4–5. Timing diagram showing how the enable line will synchronize the data transfer.

4-3: DATA BUS CONNECTION BETWEEN THE 68000 AND THE 6821

In this section of the chapter, we will discuss how the 68000 data bus is physically connected to the 6821 PIA. To begin, note that the 6821 PIA was originally designed to operate with a 6800 microprocessor. The 6800 microprocessor is an 8-bit device. The 6821 is an 8-bit peripheral device with 8 data lines.

The 68000 has 16 data lines; therefore, the data connection to the 6821 device must be to the upper 8 bits of the 68000 data bus, or the lower 8 bits. In Fig. 4-6, we have connected the 6821 to the lower-byte data lines of the 68000. It is important for the system software to know which half of the system data bus the PIA is connected to. When data is transmitted to or received from the I/O device, the 68000 must be informed electrically of which byte of the data bus the data will be input on. This point will be emphasized when we show the 68000 software to control the 6821 PIA.

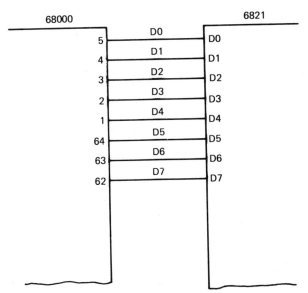

FIGURE 4–6. Schematic diagram showing the 68000 lower byte data lines connected to the data input lines for the 6821.

4-4:   ADDRESS CONNECTION TO THE 6821

Let us now discuss how the 68000 address lines will connect to the 6821 PIA. There are two physical address lines from the 68000 that will connect directly to the 6821. These address lines are A1 and A2. Recall that there is no external A0 address line on the 68000 device.

The address lines A1 and A2 will physically connect to the RS0 and RS1 input lines on the 6821. (See Fig. 4-7.) With the address lines connected in this way, the register select for the 6821 will be accomplished by A1 and A2 being set to all possible logical combinations.

In a byte type of addressing scheme, this would mean that A0 would be included. However, A0 is not external to the CPU. The logical combinations for the byte addressing is as follows;

A2	A1	A0	PIA REGISTER
0	0	0	Register 0 D8–D15
0	0	1	Register 0 D0–D7
0	1	0	Register 1 D8–D15
0	1	1	Register 1 D0–D7
1	0	0	Register 2 D8–D15
1	0	1	Register 2 D0–D7
1	1	0	Register 3 D8–D15
1	1	1	Register 3 D0–D7

From the preceding list, we can see that it is possible to select any of the four internal registers on the PIA and set the A0 bit to a logical 1 or a logical 0. When communicating with the 8-bit device, it is important to know which data lines the device is connected to. If the device is connected to the lower-byte data lines, then all odd addresses, 1, 3, 5 and 7, are used to address the PIA registers 0, 1, 2, and 3. If the PIA is connected to the upper-byte data lines, then all even addresses, 0, 2, 4 and 6 are used to select the PIA registers 0, 1, 2, and 3.

4-5:   CHIP SELECT FOR THE 6821

Now that we know how the RS0 and RS1 inputs are connected to the address bus, let us consider the question of how to select the chip from all the possible address space. In Chap. 3, we discussed the

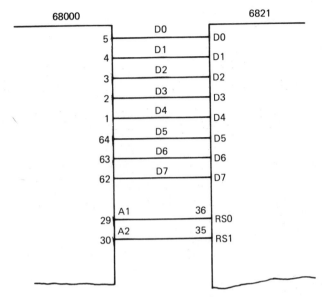

FIGURE 4–7. Schematic diagram showing the 68000 address line A1 and A2 connected to RS0 and RS1 of the 6821 devices.

memory-mapped I/O architecture of the 68000. Therefore, we must map the 6821 device into the system memory space.

There are a number of classical techniques for mapping an I/O device into a system memory space. For ease of illustration, we will use a very simple one. We will assume that when the address line A23 is a logical 1, we are communicating with I/O. (Refer to Chap. 3.)

To divide this I/O space further, we will say that when A23 is a logical 1 and A21 is a logical 1, the 6821 is selected to communicate with the CPU. This type of architecture can be thought of as memory-mapped, linear select—that is, our I/O space is memory-mapped and the I/O space is divided up in a linear select fashion. Each possible I/O device is assigned a single address line A1–A22 for enable.

Figure 4-8 shows the connection of the A21 and A23 address lines to enable the device. Notice in Fig. 4-8 that both A23 and A21 must be a logical 1 in order for CS0 and CS1 to become a logical 1. We have not shown how the $\overline{CS2}$ signal is set.

When decoding the 8-bit peripheral device, use can be made of the $\overline{UDS}$ and $\overline{LDS}$ output lines from the 68000. If the 8-bit device is connected to the upper 8 bits of the data bus, $\overline{UDS}$ may be used to provide a qualifying signal. If the peripheral device is connected to

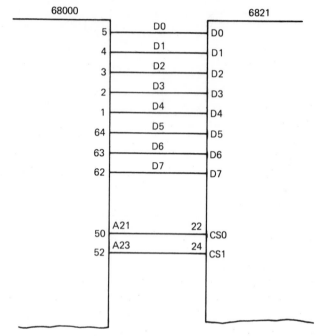

FIGURE 4–8. Schematic diagram showing the 68000 address lines connected to the CS0 and CS1 chip select inputs of the 6821.

the lower 8 bits of the data bus, $\overline{\text{LDS}}$ may be used to provide a qualifying signal.

In 6800-type operations, $\overline{\text{UDS}}$ and $\overline{\text{LDS}}$ do not strobe data. These control lines can be thought of as $\overline{\text{UDS}}$ = A0 and $\overline{\text{LDS}}$ = $\overline{\text{A0}}$. You must be concerned with these signals if two 8-bit peripherals are connected to the upper and lower data byte at the same I/O address. When $\overline{\text{UDS}}$ is a logical 0, the CPU will communicate with the upper byte device. When $\overline{\text{LDS}}$ is a logical 0, the CPU will communicate with the lower byte device. (See Fig. 4-9.)

When using only the upper byte or lower byte at a specific address, the correct software address can be used to inform the 68000 where the data is coming from or going to. No hardware select is necessary.

4-6:   USING THE VPA INPUT ON THE 68000

The 68000 CPU device is capable of operating at clock speeds up to 10 megahertz. The 6821 PIA device is capable of operating at speeds near 1 megahertz and slower. Most 6800 peripheral devices

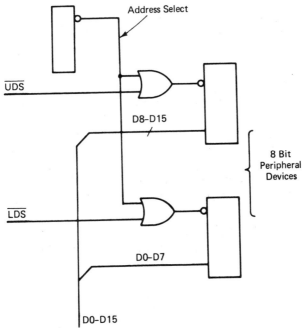

FIGURE 4–9. When $\overline{UDS}$ is a logical 0 the upper byte is enabled. When $\overline{LDS}$ is a logical 0 the lower byte device is enabled.

were designed to operate at speeds close to 1 megahertz. Designers of the 68000 had the foresight to know that many users would wish to connect the 6800 peripheral devices to the 68000.

There was such a great need in the marketplace for this feature that a special function was added to the 68000 which allows this interface to occur in a straightforward manner. An input pin on the 68000 is labeled "$\overline{VPA}$." The $\overline{VPA}$ is an abbreviation for "Valid Peripheral Address." When this input is asserted in the logical 0 state, the 68000 knows electrically that the communication cycle is to be with a 6800-type peripheral device.

When the $\overline{VPA}$ input is asserted, the 68000 "syncs" up to its output line labeled "E pin 20." The E output is the input clock frequency of the 68000 on pin 15 divided by 10. When using 6800 peripheral devices with the 68000, the E output line takes on the same function as the Phase 2 clock in 6800-based systems.

Figure 4-10 illustrates the schematic diagram of how we will assert the $\overline{VPA}$ input to the 68000. In Fig. 4-10, the proper address space is decoded and must be qualified by the $\overline{AS}$ output line from the 68000. This will ensure that the 68000 receives the $\overline{VPA}$ input at the proper time in the communication cycle.

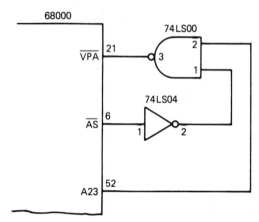

FIGURE 4–10. Schematic diagram showing how the *VPA* input to the 68000 will be asserted during a 6800 type of data transfer. Notice that the $\overline{VPA}$ input is synchronized to the *AS* bar output of the 68000.

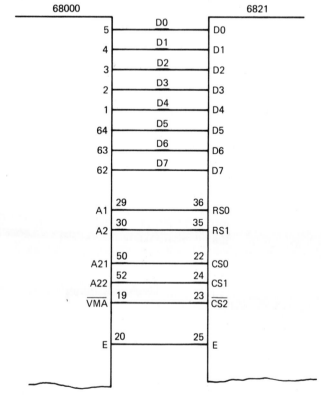

FIGURE 4–11. Schematic diagram showing how the *E* (enable) line from the 68000 device is connected to the 6821 *E* input line.

In the 6821 interface, the E clock output line on the 68000 is connected to the ENABLE input line pin 25 on the 6821. (See Fig. 4-11.)

Another important signal on the 68000 that is used for interface with 6800 peripheral devices is labeled "$\overline{\text{VMA}}$." Readers who are familiar with 6800-based systems understand the function of the $\overline{\text{VMA}}$ output pin on the 6800. This output was used to inform the external hardware in a 6800 system that a "Valid Memory Address" was present on the 6800 address bus. The system hardware would qualify the chip select decoding with the $\overline{\text{VMA}}$ output line.

In the 68000 system, the $\overline{\text{VMA}}$ output line electrically indicates that the 68000 is outputting a valid 6800-type communication. This signal should be used to qualify the 6800 peripheral chip select address. Whenever the 68000 is outputting a system address during a 6800 cycle, the $\overline{\text{VMA}}$ output line is a logical 0. For the 6821, we will connect the $\overline{\text{VMA}}$ output line on the 68000, pin 19, to the CS2 input line, pin 23, on the PIA. Figure 4-12 shows the connections between the 68000 and the 6821 that we have discussed thus far.

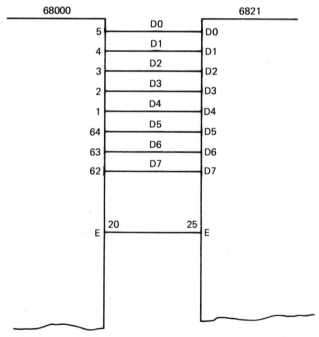

FIGURE 4–12. Complete schematic diagram showing the connections we have discussed between the 68000 and the 6821 device.

4-7: CONNECTION OF THE R/W LINE

The 68000 device has a single R/$\overline{W}$ output line, pin 9. When this line is a logical 1, the CPU will be reading data. When the R/$\overline{W}$ is a logical 0, the CPU will be writing data. These are the same logical levels that the 6821 device responds to with its R/$\overline{W}$ input line, pin 21. Therefore, we can connect the R/$\overline{W}$ output line from the 68000 to the 6821 R/$\overline{W}$ input, pin 21, of the 6821. Figure 4-13 shows a complete interface between the 68000 and the 6821.

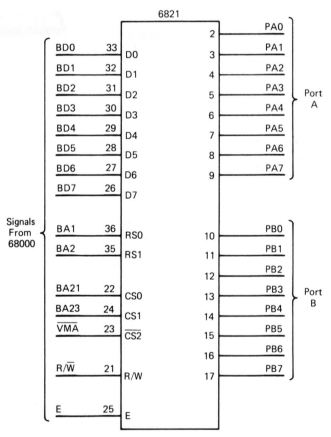

FIGURE 4–13.   Schematic diagram of the complete electrical interface between the 68000 and the 6821 *PIA*.

4-8: TIMING DIAGRAMS FOR COMMUNICATION WITH THE 6821

Figures 4-14 and 4-15 show general timing diagrams for READ and WRITE operations between the 6821 and the 68000.

4-9: SEQUENCE OF ELECTRICAL EVENTS FOR A 6800-TYPE READ

In this section of the chapter, we present the general sequence of electrical events that occurs during a READ operation for the 68000 during communication with a 6800-type peripheral device. This sequence is important to understand as a first-level approximation for the interface of 6800-type peripheral devices. From this general sequence of events, the system data sheets can be studied to obtain the necessary timing details. These details are necessary, but

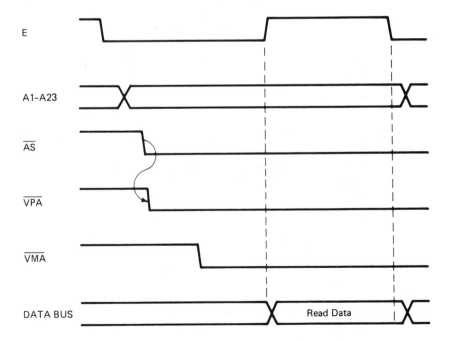

R/W = Logical 1

FIGURE 4–14. Timing diagram of a general I/O *READ* operation for a 6800 type of I/O cycle with the 68000.

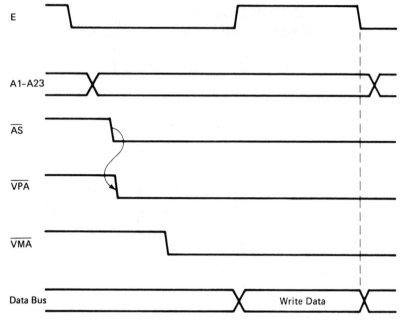

FIGURE 4–15.   Timing diagram of a general I/O *WRITE* operation for a 6800 type of I/O cycle with the 68000.

difficult to comprehend if you do not have a good general idea of what should occur during the communication transfer.

The sequence for a READ operation is as follows:

1. Address lines A1–A23 are set to the peripheral address.
2. $\overline{AS}$ is asserted by the 68000.
3. $\overline{VPA}$ is input to the 68000 qualified by $\overline{AS}$.

The 68000 is now electrically aware that the communication cycle is with a 6800-type peripheral. The peripheral device will have decoded the address lines and is waiting electrically for the $\overline{VMA}$ output from the 68000 to qualify the chip select input to the peripheral device.

4. R/$\overline{W}$ is set to a logical 1, indicating to the external hardware that a READ cycle is in progress.
5. $\overline{VMA}$ is output to the system from the 68000.

The peripheral device is now electrically selected by the 68000 for communication.

6. ENABLE (E) output from the 68000 is set to a logical 1 at the correct time to synchronize the data transfer.

Data from the 6800 peripheral device is placed on the system data bus when the ENABLE output line from the 68000 is set to a logical 1. When the ENABLE output line from the 68000 goes to a logical 0, the data transfer is complete and the peripheral data is removed from the data bus.

7. The data transfer is complete. Notice that these types of data transfers are slowed down to operate at the speed of the 6800-type peripheral device.

4-10: SEQUENCE OF EVENTS FOR A 6800-TYPE WRITE

The following sequence of electrical events will occur during a WRITE operation from the 68000 to a 6800-type peripheral device.

1. Address lines A1–A23 are set to the peripheral address of the 6800-type device.
2. $\overline{AS}$ is asserted by the 68000.
3. $\overline{VPA}$ is input to the 68000 by external hardware.

The 68000 is now electrically informed that the bus communication will be with a 6800-type peripheral device.

4. R/$\overline{W}$ is set to a logical 0 by the 68000.
5. $\overline{VMA}$ is asserted to a logical 0 by the 68000.

Next, the peripheral device will use the $\overline{VMA}$ output to qualify the chip select circuits.

6. The 68000 outputs the data to write to the peripheral device on the 68000 data bus. The data is physically on the upper or lower data lines.
7. ENABLE output from the 68000 is set to a logical 1 at the correct time.

The ENABLE signal will synchronize the data transfer from the 68000 to the 6800-type peripheral device. The output data is latched into the 6800-type device on the high to low transition of this signal. This is exactly the same operation that would occur if the peripheral device were used in a system that was 6800-based and had a Phase 2 clock input.

8. The data transfer is complete when the ENABLE line from the 68000 transfers from a logical 1 to a logical 0.

4-11: DIFFERENCES BETWEEN 68000 I/O AND 6800 I/O

In this section, we will discuss some of the differences in I/O operations with the 68000. When the 68000 is communicating with 68000-type I/O devices, the transfer is exactly the same as with memory. (This was discussed in Chap. 3.) We will concentrate on the differences encountered when the 68000 is communicating with 6800-type peripheral devices.

The first difference we note is the lack of use of the $\overline{\text{DTACK}}$ input to the 68000 during a 6800-type bus cycle. Recall that the $\overline{\text{DTACK}}$ input to the 68000 informed the processor electrically that the source or destination for the data was ready to proceed in the transfer cycle. In a 6800-type cycle, there is no need for the peripheral device to assert this input. The $\overline{\text{DTACK}}$ input is a logical 1 during a 6800-type data transfer. The specifications for the 68000 indicate that the $\overline{\text{DTACK}}$ input must be a logical 1 during a 6800 I/O cycle. This means that the external hardware must ensure that the $\overline{\text{DTACK}}$ is not asserted when the $\overline{\text{VPA}}$ input is active.

The next difference between a 6800- and 68000-type cycle is in the use of the output lines $\overline{\text{UDS}}$ and $\overline{\text{LDS}}$. During a 6800-type cycle, both of these outputs are asserted in a similar way to address lines. $\overline{\text{UDS}}$ = 0 when the address is even, and $\overline{\text{LDS}}$ = 0 when the address is odd. Both of these lines equal a logical 0 if a word operation is specified by the system software.

During a 68000 I/O operation, the $\overline{\text{UDS}}$ and $\overline{\text{LDS}}$ output lines are used to isolate the upper and lower data bytes and supply the data strobe. In a 6800-type operation, the peripheral device must use the ENABLE signal to strobe data.

4-12: SOFTWARE FOR CONTROLLING A 6821 PIA

In this section of the chapter, we will show the software required to control the 6821 device to act in three different ways. These ways will be:

1. Both ports are output.
2. Both ports are input.
3. One port is output, one port is input.

When reviewing the software program, it will be seen that very few changes take place from example to example. We will make use of the information given in Section 4-2 on the general operation of the PIA. It will also be assumed that the PIA is connected to the 68000, as shown in Fig. 4-13.

Note that, in the software, word operations are specified to communicate with the peripheral device. During word operations, the data is always located in the lower byte. An example follows on pages 92–97.

4-13:   CHAPTER SUMMARY

We discussed in this chapter the basics of input and output operations between the 68000 and 6800-type peripheral devices. The discussion started with an overview of the 6821 device. In this overview, we presented information concerning how the device must be communicated with.

Next, the hardware interface between the 6821 and the 68000 was shown. Each input pin of the 6821 was discussed and connected to an appropriate pin of the 68000. We then discussed differences between I/O operations with 6800- and 68000-type peripherals.

Finally, an example was given of 68000 software for electrical communication with the 6821 device. After studying the information presented in this chapter, you should have a good idea of how to interface most 6800-type peripheral devices to the 68000, 16-bit microprocessor.

ASMB,L

```
 2
 3   *********************************************************************
 4*
 5*
 6*   68000 PROGRAM TO CONTROL THE 6821 PERIPHERAL DEVICE
 7*   A23 = 1 DESIGNATES I/O SPACE
 8*   A21 = 1 DESIGNATES 6821 SELECTED
 9*
10*   SELECT CODES FOR THE 6821 ARE
11*
12*   A00000 = REGISTER 0   RS0 = 0, RS1 = 0
13*   A00002 = REGISTER 1   RS0 = 1, RS1 = 0
14*   A00004 = REGISTER 2   RS0 = 0, RS1 = 1
15*   A00006 = REGISTER 3   RS0 = 1, RS1 = 1
16*
17*   THE DEVICE IS CONNECTED TO THE LOWER BYTE DATA BITS ON
18*   THE 68000 DATA BUS.
19*
20*   *********************************************************************
21*
22*
23*
24
25
26
27
28
29
30
```

```
31*
32* ************************************************************
33*
34*       THIS SECTION OF CODE WILL SET UP THE 6821 TO HAVE BOTH
35*       PARTS A AND B AS OUTPUTS
36*
37* ************************************************************
38*
39  0000  227C 0CA0 0002    MOVE.L  #0A00002,A1    SET ADD IN REG A1
40  0006  7000              MOVE    #0000H,D0      SET DATA IN REG D0
41  0008  3280              MOVE    D0,[A1]        BIT 2=0,CRA
42*
43* CONTROL REGISTER A HAS BIT 2 SET TO A LOGICAL 0. THIS
44* INDICATES THAT WE HAVE ACCESS TO THE DATA
45* DIRECTION CONTROL REGISTER
46*
47  000A  207C 00A0 0000    MOVE.L  #0A00000,A0    SET ADD IN REG A0
48  0010  303C 00FF         MOVE    #00FFH,D0      SET DATA IN D0
49  0014  3080              MOVE    D0,[A0]        SET PA TO OUTPUT
50*
51* WE HAVE JUST PROGRAMMED THE DATA OUTPUT LINES IN
52* PA AS OUTPUTS. NOW TO SET THE CONTROL REGISTER
53* TO ALLOW ACCESS TO THE PA LINES FROM THE PROCESSOR.
54*
55  0016  7004              MOVE.Q  #04H,D0        SET BIT 2=1 IN CRA
56  0018  3280              MOVE    D0,[A1]
57*
58* DONE WITH PORT A
59*
```

(continued)

93

ASMB,L

```
60*
61*              NOW TO SET UP PORT B AS AN OUTPUT
62   001A  267C  00A0  0006   MOVE.L  #0A00006,A3    SET ADD OF PIA, REG
63   0020  7000               MOVE    #0000H,D0      SET BIT 2 OF CRB
64   0022  3640               MOVE    D0, [A3]
65*
66*              NOW TO SET THE DATA DIRECTION
67*
68   0024  247C  00A0  0004   MOVE.L  #0A00004H,A2   SET ADD OF PIA, REG
69   002A  303C  00FF         MOVE    #00FFH,D0      SET DATA IN REG DO
70   002E  3480               MOVE    D0, [A2]       PROGRAM OUTPUTS PB
71*
72*              ALL OUTPUTS OF PB HAVE BEEN SET
73*              NOW TO SET UP THE DEVICE TO GET
74*              ACCESS TO PB FROM THE PROCESSOR
75*
76   0030  7004               MOVE.Q  #04H,D0
77   0032  3680               MOVE    D0, [A3]       SET BIT 2=1 IN CB
78*
79*
80*              NOW BOTH PORTS ARE SET UP TO OUTPUT DATA
81*
82*              THE NEXT SECTION WILL SET PORT A
83*              DATA OUTPUT TO 55 AND PORT B
84*              DATA OUTPUT TO 97 IN HEX.
85*
86   0034  7055               MOVE.Q  #55H,D0
87   0036  3080               MOVE    D0, [A0]
88   0038  303C  0097         MOVE    #0097H,D0      WRITE DATA TO PA
```

```
89   003C  3480   MOVE     D0, [A2]    WRITE DATA TO PB
90*
91*         END OF THIS SET UP EXAMPLE
92*
93*
94*         IN THIS NEXT EXAMPLE WE WILL SET UP BOTH PORTS
95*         AS INPUT PORTS.
96*
97*         THIS SECTION OF THE PROGRAM WILL ASSUME THAT
98*
99*         A0 = PIA REG 0
100*        A1 = PIA REG 1
101*        A2 = PIA REG 2
102*        A3 = PIA REG 3
103*
104*
105*
106  003E  7000   MOVE.Q   #00H,D0     SET D0 = 0
107  0040  3280   MOVE     D0, [A1]    SET BIT 2=0,CRA
108  0042  3080   MOVE     D0, [A0]    ALL PA = INPUTS
109*
110*
111*         PORT A IS NOW SET UP
112*
113  0044  3680   MOVE     D0, [A3]    SET BIT 2=0,CRB
114  0046  3480   MOVE     D0, [A2]    ALL PB = INPUTS
115*
116*         PORT B IS NOW SET UP
117*
118  0048  7004   MOVE.Q   #04H,D0
```

(continued)

95

ASMB,L

```
119    004A    3280            MOVE     D0, [A1]        BIT 2=1,CRA
120    004C    3680            MOVE     D0, [A3]        BIT 2=1,CRB
121*
122*         BOTH PORTS ARE NOW READY TO INPUT DATA
123*
124    004E    3210            MOVE     [A0], D1        INPUT DATA FROM PA
125    0050    3412            MOVE     [A2], D2        INPUT DATA FROM PB
126*
127*         END OF THIS EXAMPLE
128*
129*
130*         IN THIS NEXT EXAMPLE PORT A WILL BE SET UP
131*         AS AN OUTPUT PORT AND PORT B WILL BE SET UP
132*         AS AN INPUT PORT. WE WILL ASSUME THE SAME
133*         DEFINITIONS FOR A0-A3.
134*
135    0052    7000            MOVE.Q   #00H,D0
136    0054    3280            MOVE     D0, [A1]        BIT 2=0,CRA
137    0056    3680            MOVE     D0, [A3]        BIT 2=0,CRB
138*
139    0058    3480            MOVE     D0, [A2]        PB = INPUT
140    005A    303C    00FF    MOVE     #00FFH,D0
141    005E    3080            MOVE     D0, [A0]        PA = OUTPUT
142*
143*         BOTH PORTS HAVE NOW BEEN SET
144*
145    0060    7004            MOVE.Q   #04H,D0
146    0062    3280            MOVE     D0, [A1]        BIT 2=1,CRA
```

```
147    0064    3680    MOVE      D0, [A3]      BIT 2=1,CRB
148*
149*   THE PIA IS NOW READY TO OUTPUT DATA
150*   AT PORT A AND INPUT DATA FROM PORT B
151*
152    0066    7048    MOVE.Q    #48H,D0       OUTPUT 48 TO PA
153    0068    3040    MOVE      D0, [A0]
154    006A    3212    MOVE      [A2], D1      INPUT PB TO D1
155*
156*   END OF ALL EXAMPLES FOR THE 6821
157*
158*
159*
160    006C    0000    END
```

CHAPTER 5

STATIC STIMULUS TESTING FOR THE 68000

5-1: INTRODUCTION

In this chapter, the basics of the hardware troubleshooting technique called Static Stimulus Testing (SST) will be discussed. The technique was first formalized in the textbook *Understanding and Troubleshooting the Microprocessor,* (Prentice-Hall, Inc., 1980). Static Stimulus Testing, originally developed as a troubleshooting technique for 8-bit microprocessor systems in industry, was born out of a need to repair and debug microprocessor systems that fell into two main categories:

1. Systems that have experienced some type of catastrophic failure and cannot execute any software; these are systems that once worked but do not work now.

2. Systems that are in a prototype mode and have never worked; these are systems that have not yet been debugged, or the software is not complete and therefore cannot be used in the diagnostic process. In these systems, the hardware designer or troubleshooter wishes to verify proper operation of all, or part, of the hardware design without using the system software.

In both of these cases, classical hardware troubleshooting techniques such as Logic State Analysis and Signature Analysis are of little help. Both of these hardware techniques require that the system be capable of executing some software in order for the technique to be of use. There are new techniques being developed for Signature Analysis that will not put dependence on software. However, there is still a large gap to be filled in the area of troubleshooting microprocessor systems. The question to be answered is this: "Where and how do I start to repair a system that is totally inoperative? That is, how do I fix a system that will not execute any system software diagnostics?"

Static Stimulus Testing, although still in its infancy, does indeed bridge that gap. Using the SST approach, you always have a starting point in debugging the system hardware. With SST, you can debug an inoperative system in a direct and orderly fashion to a point where the software diagnostics can be run. Using simple and inexpensive instruments, this can be accomplished in an efficient and straightforward manner.

An important feature of SST is the total independence of system software for it to be used. This means that a skilled hardware person, technician, or engineer can apply SST with little training in any system software! This fact becomes a major plus for the person who must service the equipment in the field and for the person who has not had extensive software training.

In this text, the SST techniques will be used to verify the entire hardware of a system. It will be assumed that the software does not exist. This is analogus to a prototype system that has just been constructed and in which one wishes to verify the hardware operation. Or, this can be exactly like a system that has malfunctioned and for which one does not have a software listing or one's knowledge of the system software is minimal. The main thrust and problem is that we need to verify the hardware without regard to the software.

As each section of the system hardware is verified using the SST, you will begin to develop a "feel" for what is occurring in the system. From these discussions, you will further understand how the 68000 communicates electrically in a system environment. Finally, using the examples given, you will see how any malfunctioning microprocessor system, 8- or 16-bit, can be approached and debugged in a straightforward manner.

5-2:   OVERVIEW OF STATIC STIMULUS TESTING

The main concept underlying Static Stimulus Testing is that electrical communication within a microprocessor system is essentially *static* in nature—that is, there are two voltage levels representing 1's and 0's. In operation, a microprocessor system alternates between these two basically static states. The electrical events usually take place in rapid succession, but they do not have to. The fact is, there is an upper limit to how fast the system can operate, and there is no lower limit. Communications between the microprocessor and memory, and between the microprocessor and I/O, are electrically static operations.

The signal lines of the microprocessor system are performing a unique electrical function at any given time in the operation. If the system were electrically "frozen" in time, one could then statically verify the logical condition of all signal lines, one at a time.

During a memory communication, for example, the system address lines are logically pointing to a particular memory location. This action is occurring regardless of the logical state of any other system signals.

USING SST, ONE CAN TREAT EACH SIGNAL LINE IN THE SYSTEM AS AN INDEPENDENT LOGIC SIGNAL.

Each system signal always has a point of electrical origin and a point of electrical destination. This is always true. Using SST as the source, a single signal line can be forced to a desired logical condition at the point of origin. With the input signal at a particular logic level, the electrical response of the line can be traced.

THE ELEMENT OF TIME-DEPENDENT SIGNALS IS ELIMINATED WITH SST.

Using standard digital troubleshooting techniques and SST, the hardware of a microprocessor system can be debugged simply. Once the dynamic situation has been transformed into a static one, it becomes a much easier problem to solve. This is true regardless of the complexity of the system hardware. SST techniques can be used to verify the entire system hardware operation.

We note, too, that SST will work in a system where special LSI devices, such as PIAs (Programmable Interface Adapters) or ACIAs (Asyncronous Communication Interface Adapters), are used. In these instances, the basic foundation of SST is still valid. This is due to the fundamental theme that all microprocessor communication in the system is static.

You may argue that dynamic RAMs are not static devices. While this is essentially true, it must be qualified. The only part of the dynamic RAM system that is dynamic is the storage cell of the memory. All addressing inputs, $\overline{RAS}$, $\overline{CAS}$, and multiplexing of addresses can be thought of as static operations. It is true that the memory cell itself will not operate in the static mode, but using a static approach will allow debugging of all of the peripheral signals of the memory system.

To illustrate the main point of SST, let us give an example. In our example, the address inputs to the system ROM will be checked. Please note that detailed procedures for the 68000 will be presented

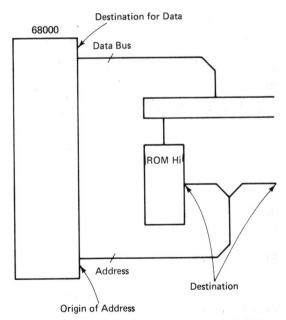

FIGURE 5–1. Simplified block diagram showing the major blocks associated with the microprocessor and the system *ROM.*

later in the text. For now, our main objective is to explain the concept of SST applied to a real system.

Figure 5-1 shows a block diagram of a microprocessor system. Also shown in Fig. 5-1 is the point of origin and termination for the address of system ROM. In this example, we wish to verify proper hardware operation of these address lines using SST. To accomplish our objective, the following general procedures are given.

1. Remove the microprocessor from the system. Install a cable that is connected to the SST switch panel. (See Fig. 5-2.)

2. Let us assume that we have a switch for every address line A1–A23. Each switch can force one line to either a logical 1 or a logical 0. These 23 switches may be set by the operator to any of the different possible logical combinations.

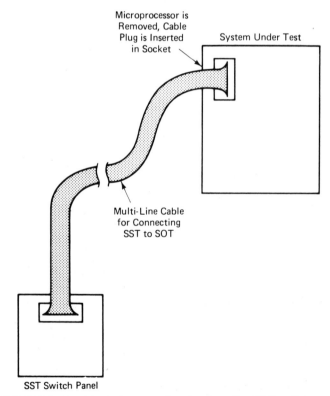

Microprocessor is Removed, Cable Plug is Inserted in Socket

System Under Test

Multi-Line Cable for Connecting SST to SOT

SST Switch Panel

FIGURE 5–2. Block diagram showing how the *SST* switch panel connects to the microprocessor system under test. Notice that the system microprocessor is removed and the *SST* cable is installed in the vacated socket.

3. The combination that is set on the address switches can be left indefinitely (*static*). Now, the input to the address buffers in a 68000 system can be verified using static dc measurement techniques. The operator can now determine if all points along these lines are the same (proper) logical condition that was set on the switches of the SST.

4. Next, a switch can be used to set the $\overline{AS}$ control signal to a logical 0. At this point, the outputs of the address latches, if used, will be equal to the input lines A1–A23 that were set using the address switches. If no address latches are used, then the $\overline{AS}$ switches need not be asserted.

5. The logical voltage levels of the address lines are now examined at the ROM address inputs. These lines can be examined with an oscilliscope, logic probe, DVM, or any dc measurement tool.

In this general example, only the address lines were discussed. It is possible to examine the address lines separately because SST creates an independence of system signals. Further, note that there was no mention of absolute time. The emphasis is on the sequence of electrical events. One may take as long as necessary to trace a particular signal from its origin to its destination.

In the troubleshooting chapters that follow, many detailed explanations and examples of how SST may be used to verify the 68000 system hardware will be given.

5-3: HARDWARE FOR THE STATIC STIMULUS TESTER

The SST that will be used in this text is a very simple hardware device. It is well-suited to educational purposes as well as to industry. The central theme for the instrument operation is "static control by the operator of the logic level of any system signal line that the microprocessor would normally control." For the 68000, these signal lines are:

A1–A23, $\overline{AS}$, $\overline{UDS}$, $\overline{LDS}$, R/$\overline{W}$, E, $\overline{VMA}$, FCO, FC1, FC2, $\overline{BG}$.

The other 68000 device pins are input that provide voltages and data which the microprocessor acts on. We will discuss these device pins in a later section of this chapter. A key point about SST that has not been mentioned is the troubleshooting technique.

"WILL BREAK ALL FEEDBACK LOOPS IN THE SYSTEM"

Let us go through the design of the SST hardware, making use of the information that has been given thus far in the chapter. This will be beneficial to understanding how to use and modify the SST to fit a particular application. Further, the discussion will show the simplicity of this particular hardware debugging technique.

5-4: STIMULUS FOR A1–A23

Figure 5-3 shows the block diagram for the hardware required to realize the address stimulus of the SST. In that figure, the logical value of the address output is determined by the physical position of the DIP switches. The output of the switch is logically inverted and buffered. Buffers used for this hardware task are capable of tri-state control, the reason for which will be discussed later in this chapter. For now, it should be noted that the address buffers can be tri-stated. Figure 5-4 shows the actual hardware schematic for realization of the address stimulus.

5-5: STIMULUS FOR FC0–FC2

The physical stimulus for the status lines of the 68000 is accomplished in exactly the same way as the address stimulus. Figure 5-5 shows the schematic diagram for the hardware required. In that

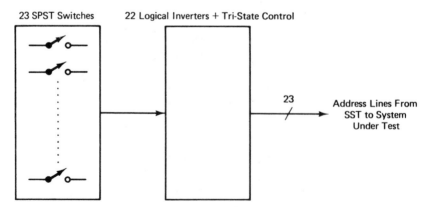

FIGURE 5–3. Block diagram showing major hardware blocks used for realizing the address stimulus in the *SST*.

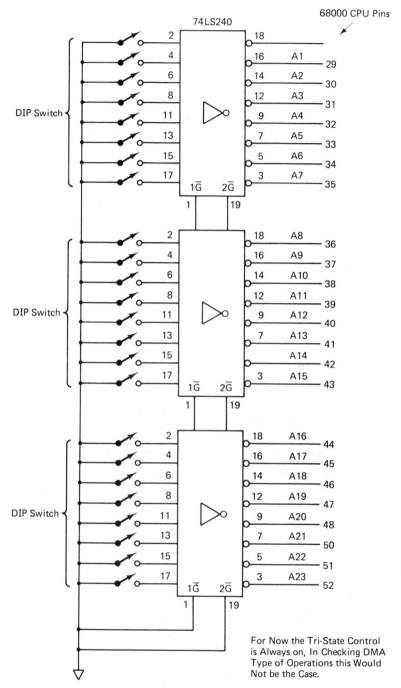

FIGURE 5–4. Schematic diagram showing how the address lines A1–A23 can be electrically stimulated in the *SST*.

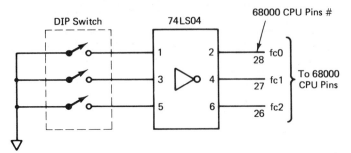

FIGURE 5–5. Schematic diagram showing how the status lines FC0–FC2 can be electrically controlled in the *SST.*

figure, the output of the DIP switches is inverted and buffered. There is no tri-state control used for the status output lines.

In the actual 68000 system the status lines are capable of tri-state operation. For the manual SST in this application, tri-stating of the status lines is not necessary. If one wishes the line to be tri-stated, the 7404 can be removed from its socket to achieve the desired isolation between its inputs and outputs, or a tri-state inverter can be used.

We have not discussed the function of the status output on the 68000. These outputs logically indicate the type of operation that is in progress during 68000 operation. For an exact definition of the status lines, refer to the data sheet on the 68000 in the Appendix.

5-6: STIMULUS FOR $\overline{\text{AS}}$, R/$\overline{\text{W}}$, $\overline{\text{UDS}}$, $\overline{\text{LDS}}$, $\overline{\text{BG}}$, E, $\overline{\text{VMA}}$

The discussion will now center on how to generate the following control signals on the SST:

$$\overline{\text{AS}},\ \overline{\text{UDS}},\ \overline{\text{LDS}},\ \text{R/}\overline{\text{W}},\ \overline{\text{BG}},\ \text{E},\ \overline{\text{VMA}}.$$

All of these signals are discussed in the same section because the hardware required for each is identical. These signals are control lines generated by the 68000 and are output to the system. Most are valid at the start of a memory cycle and stay valid during the entire cycle. Others are used to strobe data or synchronize a data transfer. To generate these signals, SPDT toggle switches are used for the stimulus. Outputs of the switches are input to switch debounce circuits. Debounce circuit outputs are used as the final outputs to the system under test. (Figure 5-6 shows the schematic for generation of these control signals.)

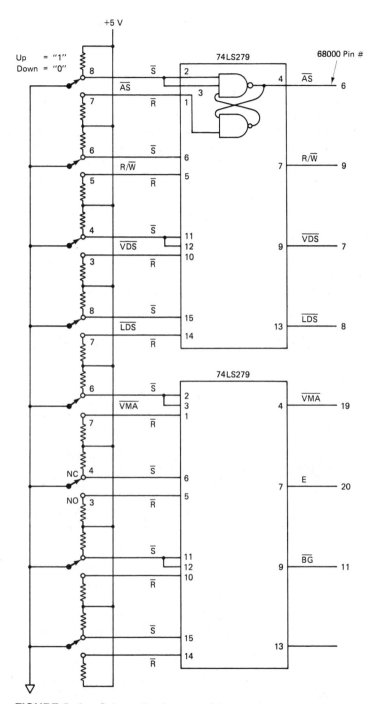

FIGURE 5–6. Schematic diagram of the hardware necessary to debounce all major control signals generated by the 68000. The 74LS279 device has four debounce, set, reset, latches internal to it. The switches used are *SPDT* toggle switches.

The schematic of Fig. 5-6 makes use of the 74279 Integrated Circuit. This device contains four SET (S)–RESET (R) latches. These latches are used as the debounce circuit for the switches.

5-7:   DATA STIMULUS FOR THE 68000 SST

In this section, we will discuss how the 68000 data lines D0–D15 are electrically stimulated by the SST. Figure 5-7 shows the schematic diagram for the data stimulus.

We see in Fig. 5-7 that each data output line is controlled by a SPST, DIP switch. One side of the switch is connected to ground potentials; the other side of the switch is connected to an input pin on the 74LS240, IC1 or IC2. When the switch is open, the input line to the 74LS240 will float to an open input level. This level is electrically treated as a logical 1 by the 74LS240.

When the switch is closed, the input voltage level to the 74LS240 is a logical 0. By inputting either a logical 1 or a logical 0 to the 74LS240, the output line will be switched from a logical 0 to a logical 1. In this way, the user has complete control over the logical output level of a data line.

In Fig. 5-7 the enable line, pin 1, 19 of the 74LS240, IC1 and IC2, is connected to the R/$\overline{\text{W}}$ line of the 68000. This will allow the data output buffers to be disabled during a READ operation. This is exactly the same type of hardware event that occurs internally on the 68000 device. During a READ operation, other system hardware besides the 68000 will be controlling the data bus lines.

5-8:   LED DISPLAY FOR THE 68000 DATA BUS

The next circuit to discuss for the SST hardware is the one that will visually examine the logical state of the data bus. This visual examination can be accomplished by using 16 LEDs to display the logical condition of each line for the system data bus. Figure 5-7 shows how this display is realized. Here, the microprocessor (or SST) data bus is connected to the inputs of the 74LS240 inverters. The outputs of these devices drive the LEDs. A logical 0 on the inputs of the 74LS240 will turn the LEDs off. A logical 1 on the inputs of the 74LS240 will turn the LEDs on.

The LEDs will reflect the logical condition of the signal lines at the microprocessor device pins D0–D15. This allows one actually to

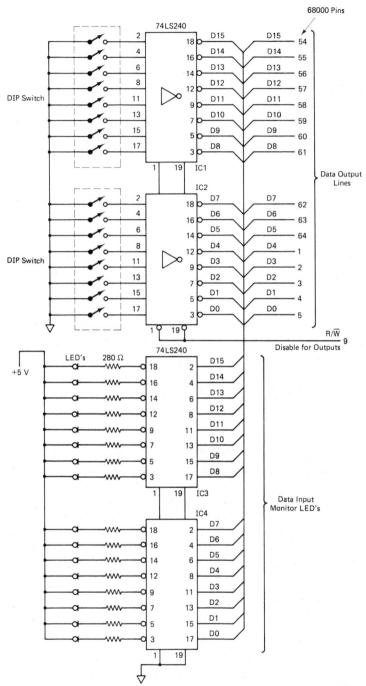

FIGURE 5–7. Schematic diagram showing the circuit for electrical stimulus of the 68000 data lines and the electrical monitoring of the 68000 data lines.

see the logical value of the data being input or output by the microprocessor (SST). If two data lines are shorted, or the data is not reaching the microprocessor input pins, the data will quickly show up on the LED display.

During a WRITE operation, one can quickly see what data the 68000 (SST) is outputting to the system hardware. Notice that the display will show data directly at the device pins. This is helpful when checking the system data lines.

5-9: MONITORING OTHER INPUTS TO THE 68000

Thus far, we have discussed electrical stimulation of the address bus, data bus, and all output lines of the 68000. We have also discussed monitoring the system data bus lines. There are other 68000 input signals that may be important to monitor with the SST.

In this section, we will show a simple technique to monitor the following inputs to the 68000:

$$\overline{\text{DTACK}}, \overline{\text{IPL0}}, \overline{\text{IPL1}}, \overline{\text{IPL2}}, \overline{\text{RESET}}, \overline{\text{HALT}}, \overline{\text{VPA}}.$$

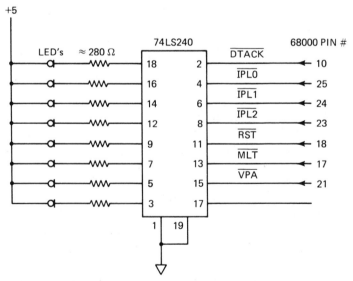

FIGURE 5–8. Schematic diagram showing the hardware required to electrically monitor the 68000 input lines that are not data.

The hardware for monitoring any of the signals that are not used in a particular system design can be eliminated. Figure 5-8 shows a schematic for the hardware required to monitor these inputs.

5-10: CHAPTER SUMMARY

In this chapter, the hardware required to realize an SST for the 68000 has been presented. You may have noticed that the hardware is not exotic. Do not be misled into believing that because the hardware is simplistic it is of little value. Nothing could be further from the truth.

In the following chapters, it will be seen what a very powerful debugging tool this simple device is for a microprocessor system. The SST can be used in prototype systems as well as in malfunctioning systems. As we shall show, it is not necessary to be a highly skilled microprocessor system designer, software person, or hardware person to achieve excellent results with the SST.

One final word: Not all of the hardware shown is necessary for the SST. If certain inputs or outputs of the 68000 are not used, then their stimulus or monitoring hardware in the SST can simply be ignored. A static stimulus tester is available from Creative Microprocessor Systems, P.O. Box 1538, Los Gatos, CA 95030.

CHAPTER 6

TROUBLESHOOTING A MEMORY READ OPERATION

In the preceding chapters, we have examined the general architecture of a 68000 system. As the architecture was discussed, exact details were given concerning the 68000 operation. In Chap. 5, we introduced the concept of Static Stimulus Testing (SST).

Beginning in this chapter and continuing through the end of the text, we will bring all of the concepts presented in the first five chapters into sharper focus. The remaining chapters will examine how to apply all of the information given thus far. First, we will discuss how to troubleshoot a memory READ operation. The troubleshooting technique used will be Static Stimulus Testing.

To show how the technique works, we will discuss troubleshooting the circuits presented in Chap. 1 through 4. In this chapter, we will be troubleshooting the hardware for a memory READ operation. This memory READ operation will be from a system ROM. However, the memory READ operation troubleshooting may be directly applicable to a system RAM as well.

It should be kept in mind that we are using the circuits in this chapter simply as a means or vehicle to transmit and illustrate the ideas of Static Stimulus Testing. All of the concepts presented here are directly applicable to other 68000 systems.

6-1: GENERAL SEQUENCE OF EVENTS FOR READING DATA FROM ROM

To start the discussion of troubleshooting a memory READ operation, we will review the sequence of events for a typical memory READ operation with the 68000. This sequence of events was given in Chap. 1 and is repeated here for the reader's convenience. The sequence is:

1. A1–A23 are set to the logical value of the system memory address from which the memory data will be read. At this point, all memory decoding is done and the proper memory devices are selected from all available memories in the system.
2. $R/\overline{W}$ is set to a logical 1. This indicates to the system hardware that a READ operation will be occurring.
3. $\overline{AS}$ is set to a logical 0 under the control of the 68000.
4. $\overline{UDS}$, $\overline{LDS}$, or both are set to a logical 0. These are the timed control signals to the external system hardware from the 68000. They indicate that the microprocessor is electrically ready to receive data. When these signals are a logical 0, the ROM data is placed on the system data bus by the system hardware. ROM data is now sent to the CPU bidirectional data buffers. From the buffers, the data are input to the 68000 microprocessor.
5. $\overline{DTACK}$ is set to a logical 0 under the control of the external hardware.
6. $\overline{LDS}$, $\overline{UDS}$, and $\overline{AS}$ are set to a logical 1 by the 68000. This action terminates the data transfer, and the ROM data is strobed into the 68000 and then electrically removed from

the system data bus. The 68000 is now ready to perform another data transfer. The new data transfer can be another memory READ or any other valid hardware operation.

The preceding summary of electrical events shows how the 68000 reads data from the system ROM. In the remainder of this chapter we will go through this general sequence of events in detail. As we examine this sequence, we will show how each event is accomplished and how the system hardware responds.

We will discuss how to verify electrically if the event is being carried out correctly. In this discussion, Static Stimulus Testing will be used extensively.

6-2:   VERIFYING THE ADDRESS BUFFERS

The first electrical event to occur in the memory READ operation is when the address lines are output from the 68000. These lines pass through address buffers before being sent to the system. (See the block diagram of Fig. 6-1.) We will discuss how to verify electrically if the address buffers are operating correctly. (The schematic for the address buffers is shown in Fig. 6-2.) Prior to performing any electrical checks in the system, we must first install the SST. This is accomplished by the following procedure:

1. Turn off all power to the 68000 system.
2. Carefully remove the 68000 from the circuit board. Install the removed 68000 microprocessor into conductive foam. This will safeguard and protect the electrical inputs from being damaged due to static charges. The foam will also

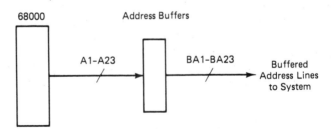

FIGURE 6–1.   Block diagram showing the concept of buffering the 68000 address lines before they are output to the system. When troubleshooting a memory *READ* operation, the address buffers must be electrically verified.

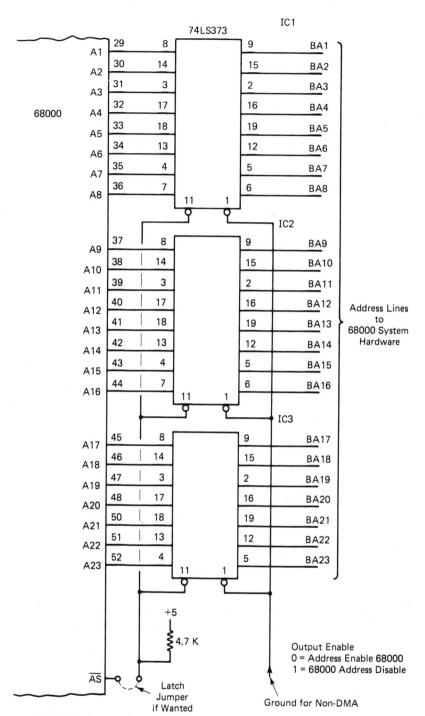

FIGURE 6–2. Schematic diagram showing one way address buffering may be realized for the 68000. Notice that this technique employs address latches. The latches may be set to the transparent mode, or they can be used as latches with *AS* as the clock input.

physically protect the pins of the 68000 Integrated Circuit from damage.

3. Install the SST cable into the socket that was vacated by the 68000 microprocessor. Care should be taken to ensure that pin 1 of the SST cable is placed into pin 1 of the socket on the 68000 board.

4. After the SST is installed, set the switches (listed below) to the unasserted position on the SST unit. The unasserted position is equivalent to the logic level all 68000 control outputs will be in when the microprocessor is starting a memory cycle. These unasserted positions for the 68000 are:

$$\overline{AS} = \text{LOGICAL 1}$$
$$\overline{LDS}, \overline{UDS} = \text{LOGICAL 1}$$
$$FC0\text{–}FC2 = \text{LOGICAL 1}$$
$$R/\overline{W} = \text{LOGICAL 1}$$
$$\overline{VMA} = \text{LOGICAL 1}$$
$$\overline{BG} = \text{LOGICAL 1}$$
$$E = \text{LOGICAL 0}$$

With these switches on the SST in these logical positions, we ensure that the unit will not cause any unwanted bus conflicts in the system.

5. Turn on the system power. Make sure that the SST also has +5 volts connected to it. The SST derives its power from the system under test.

The SST is now installed, and we are ready to proceed in the check-out of the system.

The address buffer schematic shown in Fig. 6-2 uses integrated circuits labeled "74LS373" in the realization of the address buffers. The pinout and functional block diagram for the 74LS373 is given in Fig. 6-3. We see in Fig. 6-3 that the data inputs to the 74LS373 will pass to the outputs when the enable input pin 11 is logical 1. When pin 11 goes to a logical 0, whatever logical state the output was in will be latched. The output will remain at this logical state until the enable input is again forced to a logical 1.

In the schematic of Fig. 6-2, the enable input to the 74LS373 is controlled by the $\overline{AS}$ output from the 68000 or the input is pulled to a logical 1 via the 4.7K-ohm resistor. If the input pin 11 is pulled to a logical 1, the 74LS373 will act as a simple address buffer.

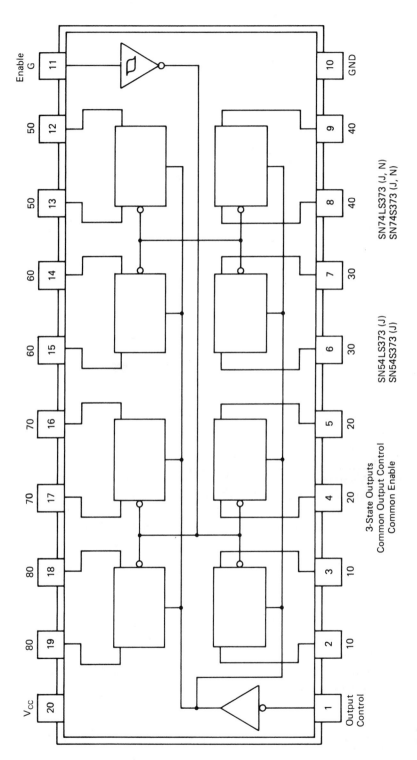

FIGURE 6–3. Block diagram showing the pinout and function of a 74LS373 Octal D-type latch.

117

To verify if the enable input to the latches is operating correctly, the following must be done:

1. Set the $\overline{\text{AS}}$ switch on the SST to a logical 0 position. The enable input pin 11 on the 74LS373 will be a logical 0. This is the HOLD mode for the latch.
2. Set the $\overline{\text{AS}}$ switch on the SST to a logical 1 position. The enable input pin 11 of the 74LS373 will now go to a logical 1. In this mode, the inputs to the device are placed on the output pins.

If the enable input to the latch does not respond correctly to the switching of the $\overline{\text{AS}}$ line on the SST, the cause must be determined before proceeding further in the system checkout procedure. If the $\overline{\text{AS}}$ output is not connected to the enable input on the 74LS373, then the preceding check may be skipped.

Let us assume that the enable input line to the 74LS373 latches responds correctly to the $\overline{\text{AS}}$ line of the SST or that the enable line is always at a logical 1 due to the pull-up resistor. We must now verify that the latches will operate correctly. To accomplish this, we will switch the address lines one at a time using the SST. As each line switches, we will monitor the output of the address buffers. The output of the buffers will reflect the change of the address input if the enable pin 11 is in the correct logical state.

6-3: PROCEDURE FOR VERIFYING THE ADDRESS LATCH (BUFFERS)

1. Set the $\overline{\text{AS}}$ switch on the SST to the logical 1 position.
2. Make sure that the $\overline{\text{UDS}}$ and $\overline{\text{LDS}}$ switches on the SST are in the logical 1 position.
3. Set the A1–A23 switches on the SST to the logical 0 position.
4. Set the A1 switch on the SST to the logical 1 position.
5. Verify that the output pin 9 of IC1 in Fig. 6-2 is a logical 1.
6. Set the A1 switch on the SST to the logical 0 position.
7. Verify that the output pin 9 of IC1 in Fig. 6-2 is a logical 0.
8. At this point, we have ensured that the A1 output of the address latch (buffer) will respond correctly to the stimulus of the A1 line on the 68000.
9. Repeat steps 3 through 8 for all address lines A2–A23.

The buffered address output and the corresponding IC pin number are given in the following list.

BUFFERED ADDRESS LINE	IC–PIN NUMBER
BA1	IC1–9
BA2	IC1–15
BA3	IC1–2
BA4	IC1–16
BA5	IC1–19
BA6	IC1–12
BA7	IC1–5
BA8	IC1–6
BA9	IC2–9
BA10	IC2–15
BA11	IC2–2
BA12	IC2–16
BA13	IC2–19
BA14	IC2–12
BA15	IC2–5
BA16	IC2–6
BA17	IC3–9
BA18	IC3–15
BA19	IC3–2
BA20	IC3–16
BA21	IC3–19
BA22	IC3–12
BA23	IC3–5

With the preceding list and the SST, we can verify that each address line will respond correctly to the stimulus by the 68000 A1–A23 outputs. All lines should respond correctly before proceeding. If any line fails to respond correctly, we may statically trace the fault using conventional digital troubleshooting techniques. The problem is one of a single digital signal that will not switch from a logical 0 to a logical 1. This problem had been solved many times before microprocessor systems were used.

We have now verified that all address lines are electrically capable of reaching the buffer outputs. In the procedure just outlined, notice that no mention of exact timing was given. The circuits were all tested using static logic. If it can be verified that the circuits will operate under static conditions, then the probability is very high that the circuits will operate under actual dynamic system conditions. If the circuits will not work under static conditions, there is no chance they will operate under dynamic conditions. The use of SST permits the verification of the system signals in the static mode.

6-4: VERIFYING THE MEMORY SELECT LINES

The next section of system hardware to verify is the memory select logic. This section of the hardware will decode the system address and enable the correct physical memory devices. The logic for this operation is shown in Fig. 6-4. We will assume in this discussion that the address outputs have been buffered and the $\overline{AS}$ control line is a logical 1.

In Fig. 6-4, IC2 of 74LS42 will electrically provide the memory enables as a function of the system address. The ROM memory space is divided into two 2K word blocks. The total word space is from 0000–1FFF. The 2K word blocks will be 0000–0FFF and

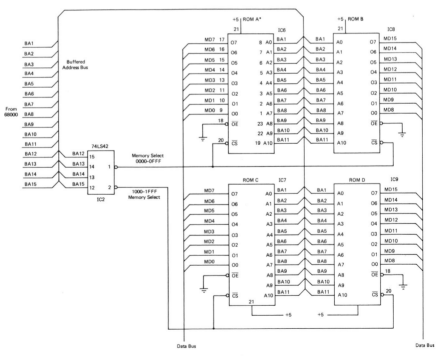

FIGURE 6–4. Partial schematic diagram showing how the memory space is decoded for the *ROM* section of system memory. The valid memory space is 000000-000FFF to 001000-001FFF.

1000–1FFF. In this discussion, we will verify that the ROM space is properly decoded.

In examining the schematic of Fig. 6-4, notice that there are four physical sockets for the ROMs. The ROMs used are actually EPROMs, 2716's, which we shall refer to simply as ROMs. These ROMs are internally organized as $2K \times 8$ bits. Therefore, it will require two of these EPROMs for each 2K word block. The 2K word block is formed using the following ICs.

ADDRESS SPACE	LOW IC	HI IC
0000–0FFF	IC6	IC8
1000–1FFF	IC7	IC9

By the terms "Low IC and Hi IC," we can define which device is connected to the lower 8 bits of the data bus and which device is connected to the upper 8 bits of the data bus, respectively. Let us now verify that all of the memory enable lines are active for the correct address space.

To verify the memory selects, the following procedure may be used. We are verifying that the $\overline{CS}$ of all four memory devices can be asserted by the 68000 with the proper address code.

6-5: PROCEDURE FOR VERIFYING THE MEMORY SELECT LINES

1. Set the address switches A1–A23 on the SST to the logical 0 position.
2. Set the $\overline{AS}$ switch on the SST to the logical 1 position.

THE ADDRESS IS NOW VALID TO THE SYSTEM

3. At this time, the memory select line for ROM space 0000–0FFF will be active.
4. With a logic probe or any dc measurement instrument, verify that pin 20 of IC6 and IC8 in Fig. 6-4 is a logical 0.
5. Verify that pin 20 of IC7 and IC9 is a logical 1.
6. Set the address switches A1–A23 on the SST to 0FFF.

THE ADDRESS SPACE IS NOW SET TO 0FFF.

7. Verify that the memory selects are still equal to the same state listed in steps 4 and 5.

Now that we have verified that the memory select lines for address space 0000–0FFF are valid, let us perform the same operation on the other two memory enable lines.

8. Set the address switches on the SST to address space 1000.

THE ADDRESS IS NOW VALID FOR SPACE 1000–1FFF.

9. Verify that pin 20 of IC7 and IC9 is a logical 0.
10. Verify that pin 20 of IC6 and IC8 is a logical 1.

It is clear from the preceding sequence of events what procedure must be followed when verifying the memory select lines. If the memory selects do not respond correctly, the system can be left set up in the static mode and the problem can be troubleshooted using standard digital troubleshooting techniques.

Note that the decoding of the memory select lines is a combinational logic problem. The system does not have to be executing at normal system speed to verify that the address space can be decoded. The system can be "frozen" in any state for as long as the user requires to troubleshoot the malfunction.

6-6: READING EPROM DATA WITH THE SST

The last hardware path that must be verified in the ROM READ operation is the data path from the 2716's back to the 68000. In step 4 of the list of events for a memory READ operation, the $\overline{\text{LDS}}$, $\overline{\text{UDS}}$, or both are set to a logical 0 by the 68000. At this time, the data from the ROM is enabled onto the system data bus and input to the 68000 data pins D0–D15. This condition can be set statically using the SST.

The LEDs on the SST will show the logical state of the data being read from the ROM. Further, we can set up the condition with the SST, stimulate the data at the ROM socket, and verify that the data will electrically reach the 68000. Both of these conditions will be covered in the following discussion.

Let us first show how to verify the memory read path shown in Fig. 6-5. We see in Fig. 6-5 the complete schematic for a 4K × 16 ROM memory. This is exactly the same schematic that was presented in Chap. 1. We will go through the sequence of events for a memory read and verify that all of the hardware of Figs. 6-5, 6-6, and 6-7 responds correctly.

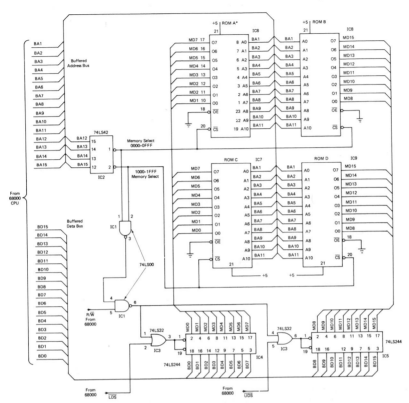

FIGURE 6-5. Complete schematic diagram of the *ROM* system that was discussed in Chapter 1 of this text.

1. First, the address lines A1–A23 are output from the 68000. We discussed how the address buffers (latches) could be verified in Section 6-3. Let us assume that the address lines are valid out of the address buffers at the CPU.

We now verify that the address lines BA1–BA11 are valid at the ROM memory address input lines. This can be verified by switching the address lines one at a time from a logical 0 to a logical 1. While switching the address line using the SST, the address input pin of the ROM can be monitored. In this fashion, it can be easily determined if all of the address lines will logically reach the ROM input lines under the control of the 68000.

2. While the address lines are present on the system address bus, the memory select lines will be decoded and asserted. Electrical verification of the memory select logic was dis-

cussed in Section 6-3. We assume that the memory address is such that the memory space from 0000–0FFF is being decoded. This means that pin 20 of IC6 and IC8 is a logical 0, while pin 20 of IC7 and IC9 is a logical 1 in Fig. 6-5.

3. Next, the R/W̄ line from the 68000 is set to a logical 1 under the control of the 68000. We see in Fig. 6-5 that the R/W̄ line is input to IC1 pin 5.

   With IC1 pin 5 a logical 1, and pin 4 a logical 1, pin 6 will be a logical 0. Pin 4 will become a logical 1, due to the output pin 1 of the 74LS42 becoming a logical 0. All of these logic conditions are static and can be verified using a logic probe or any dc measurement tool. If any of the logical conditions are not correct, the malfunction can be found using standard digital troubleshooting techniques.

   We will assume that pin 6 of IC1 in Fig. 6-5 is a logical 0, as it should be at this point in the memory read sequence.

4. The $\overline{\text{LDS}}$, the $\overline{\text{UDS}}$, or both outputs will be asserted to the logical 0 level. Several hardware actions will now occur.

   a. The first action to verify is that the memory data buffers IC4 and IC5 have their enable input pins 1 and 19 set to the logical 0 level. For this to occur, a logical 0 must be input to pins 1 and 4 of IC3 in Fig. 6-5. When $\overline{\text{UDS}}$ or $\overline{\text{LDS}}$ is set to the logical 0 level, pin 2 or pin 5 of the 74LS32, IC3 will become a logical 0. This action will set output pins 3 and 6 of IC3 to the logical 0 level. Again, we state that this action is completely static in nature.

   b. Another hardware event that will occur in the memory system is shown in Fig. 6-6. The bidirectional buffers located at the 68000 data pins will have the direction control line set to a logical 0. This is pin 19 of the 74LS245 devices. It can be verified that the direction control line is indeed a logical 0 for the device that has the $\overline{\text{UDS}}$ or $\overline{\text{LDS}}$ asserted.

   c. The third hardware event to occur when the $\overline{\text{UDS}}$ or $\overline{\text{LDS}}$ is asserted, as shown in Fig. 6-7, is the $\overline{\text{DTACK}}$ input to the 68000 will be set to a logical 0. The logical state of the $\overline{\text{DTACK}}$ input to the 68000 can be verified by visually monitoring the LED on the SST that indicates the logical condition of the $\overline{\text{DTACK}}$ input. When either the $\overline{\text{LDS}}$ output or the $\overline{\text{UDS}}$ output is asserted, the $\overline{\text{DTACK}}$ input to the 68000 will go to the logical 0 state.

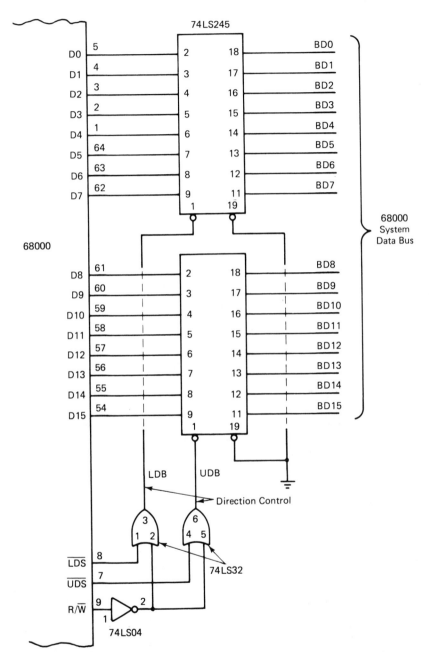

FIGURE 6–6. Schematic diagram showing the bidirectional buffering scheme used with the 68000 data lines.

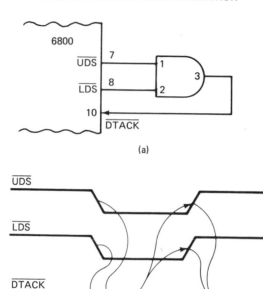

(a)

(b)

FIGURE 6–7a. Schematic diagram showing the $\overline{DTACK}$ circuit for the 68000. Notice that the $\overline{DTACK}$ input will become asserted in the logical 0 state when $\overline{UDS}$ or $\overline{LDS}$ become asserted.
FIGURE 6–7b. Timing diagram of the circuit shown in Fig. 6–7a.

All of the preceding hardware events can be electrically verified using the SST. At this point, the data from the 2716 EPROMs will be logically input to the 68000 SST.

To ensure that the correct data is being output from the ROM and reaching the SST data inputs, the software monitor listing of the ROM data at a specific address can be referred to. The hardware path that is established at this time will stay valid as long as the electrical conditions set up by the SST are valid.

The data path is from the ROM output lines to the 68000 data input lines. It is true that there is hardware between the ROM data outputs and the 68000 data inputs, but this hardware is composed of static buffers and physical bus lines. With the microprocessor system set in this condition, standard digital troubleshooting techniques may be employed to solve malfunctions.

The main point is that the troubleshooter now has enough time to examine the data, address, and control path for the system. Dynamic operation of the system has been reduced to a simpler, more easily studied and analyzed static operation.

5. The final event to occur in the memory READ sequence is the $\overline{\text{UDS}}$ and $\overline{\text{LDS}}$ control lines are set to a logical 1, under the control of the 68000. The data from the ROM is now removed from the system data bus. Memory data buffers IC4 and IC5, shown in Fig. 6-5, have their enable lines 1 and 19 set to a logical 1.

The DTACK input to the 68000 will be forced to a logical 1. Figure 6-7 shows the hardware that we discussed previously for this signal.

We have now gone through the entire sequence of events for a memory READ operation for a 68000 device. At each step in the sequence the hardware response was shown and discussed. A nice feature of SST is that each unique signal line that is asserted by the 68000 during the memory READ cycle can be asserted statically. The troubleshooter can concentrate on only one signal line of the system at a time. There is no need to examine the entire system as it is executing instructions.

In some cases, the microprocessor system is not electrically capable of executing any instructions. This is the case of a completely inoperative system, or one that has not had any software written for it. It could also be a system that is not yet totally constructed. It can be verified that a single section of the system is wired correctly and all of the logic is operative.

In the next section of this chapter, we will discuss how to stimulate the data at the EPROM socket to verify electrically the data path without knowing what data is stored in the EPROM.

6-7: STIMULATION OF THE DATA AT THE ROM SOCKET

Before a ROM is installed into a memory socket, it is useful to determine if the data at the ROM socket can electrically reach the microprocessor. Figure 6-8 shows the concept of exactly what we are trying to accomplish, using the SST. Here is how to do it. We will enable a ROM space that has empty sockets installed in the system. With this space enabled, we will ground the data output lines one at a time and monitor the response at the SST.

To achieve this, the following procedure may be used:

1. Set the address switches on the SST to an address where the sockets have had the ROMs removed. If you are bringing up

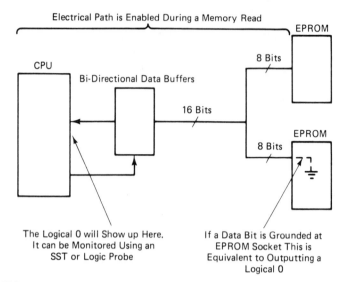

Electrical Path is Enabled During a Memory Read

EPROM

CPU

Bi-Directional Data Buffers

8 Bits

16 Bits

EPROM

8 Bits

The Logical 0 will Show up Here. It can be Monitored Using an SST or Logic Probe

If a Data Bit is Grounded at EPROM Socket This is Equivalent to Outputting a Logical 0

FIGURE 6–8. Block diagram showing the concept of stimulating data at the *EPROM* socket and sending it to the microprocessor.

a board for the first time, do not even install the ROM until this check has been performed.

2. Set the $\overline{\text{AS}}$ switch on the SST to a logical 0.

3. Set the R/$\overline{\text{W}}$ switch to a logical 1. This will electrically inform the system that a memory READ operation is in progress.

4. Set the $\overline{\text{UDS}}$ and $\overline{\text{LDS}}$ switches on the SST to a logical 0.

AT THIS TIME, THE DATA PATH FROM THE SYSTEM ADDRESS SPACE IS ENABLED TO THE MICROPROCESSOR DATA INPUT PINS D0–D15.

5. If we observe the LEDs in the SST board, all will be on. This is due to the fact that there is an empty socket where the ROM will be. The TTL inputs to the bidirectional buffers are floating. A floating TTL input is equivalent to a logical 1.

6. One at a time, we will connect the data output pins of the empty sockets to ground. Begin by connecting a ground wire to pin 9 of the empty socket IC6 of Fig. 6-5. The LED labeled "*D0*" on the SST will go off.

7. We are forcing the data at the source to a logical 0. This

logical 0 will be reflected at the destination. In this case, the destination is the 68000 data input pins.

8. This technique of grounding a data line and noting the electrical reaction of the hardware is very useful for determining if the ROM data has a "chance" of being read by the microprocessor.

You can enable any address space using this method, and determine if the data from that address space will reach the microprocessor.

6-8: CHAPTER SUMMARY

In this chapter, we have covered the details of how to verify a ROM READ operation with an SST. The sequence of events for a memory READ operation was given, and then we discussed how to simulate these events with the SST. Using the SST, the 68000 system can be set into any state of a hardware event. With the system in this state, a simple dc voltage probe can be used to troubleshoot the system effectively.

Finally, it was shown how to stimulate the data lines at the ROM socket to verify the data paths. Each data path can be verified before any physical ROMs are installed into the system. In this way, it can be determined if the system has an electrical chance of operating. If the hardware does not operate correctly in the static mode, it cannot operate correctly in the dynamic mode either.

CHAPTER 7

TROUBLESHOOTING STATIC RAM USING SST

7-1: INTRODUCTION TO THE PROBLEM

In this chapter, we will discuss how to apply Static Stimulus Testing techniques to troubleshooting a static RAM system. The two hardware operations that will be explained are reading data from RAM and writing data to RAM. The static RAM devices used for this discussion are 2114, 1K $\times$ 4, common I/O devices. In Chap. 2, we discussed how the 68000 electrically communicated with these devices. If you are unfamiliar with the 2114 memory, a review of the information presented in Chap. 2 will be of value. A data sheet of the 2114 memory is given in the Appendix.

As you examine the possible operations performed with the static RAM in a microprocessor system, the following list can be generated:

1. READ OP–CODES (ROM or RAM).
2. READ DATA stored temporarily.
3. WRITE DATA for temporary storage.
4. PUSH STACK DATA.
5. POP STACK DATA.
6. SAVE RETURN ADDRESS for subroutine.
7. RESTORE RETURN ADDRESS for subroutine.
8. SAVE RETURN VECTOR for interrupt.
9. RESTORE RETURN VECTOR for interrupt.

In examining this list, it is seen that the system RAM is communicated with at many different times when the microprocessor is executing a program. However, on closer inspection of the list we can see that when the actual RAM communication occurs, it will be either a READ or WRITE operation. The hardware of the microprocessor system does not distinguish between any of the nine memory operations listed.

The distinction between types of communications with the memory is performed by the microprocessor device. The address of RAM, data to be written to RAM, and where data will be physically stored are all taken care of by the microprocessor.

A memory device requires an address, data, and a write enable signal or read enable signal to operate correctly. The memory device has no electrical way of knowing where these signals are originating in the system and how they logically arrive at the memory inputs and outputs.

A software person must be acutely aware of most of these details. The logical formation of addresses, return vectors, and stack data are all critical points in the valid operation of a program. The hardware person cares only that, when the microprocessor wishes to write or read data electrically from memory, the memory will operate correctly. It is this tact we will take as system troubleshooters.

Each of the nine memory operations listed can be shown to be either a READ or WRITE with the system memory. Further, when the READ or WRITE occurs, it will always be performed in exactly the same way viewed from the hardware. This piece of information will greatly reduce the hardware examination that must be made to ensure that the memory is functional.

In troubleshooting the system RAM, we must ensure that the CPU is capable of reading and writing with the memory. Once we have determined that these hardware paths are electrically valid, then we may perform a test on each cell of the system memory.

If you are initially checking the system with a manual SST, a software diagnostic can be run next to test each cell of the memory system. Further, this diagnostic can output the failed memory address and the failed data bit(s) at that address location. All of this can be accomplished without the use of a system terminal or a system front panel. This diagnostic concept will be shown in Chap. 9.

7-2: SEQUENCE OF EVENTS FOR READING DATA FROM STATIC RAM

Let us concentrate on the sequence of hardware events that will occur each time data is read from static RAM with the 68000 CPU. It should be noted that the 68000 CPU has no electrical way of determining if the data is being read from static RAM or ROM. Therefore, all of the information presented in Chap. 6 on troubleshooting ROM will apply equally well to static RAM. The sequence of events for reading data from these memories is exactly the same.

We will show the sequence of events here and then discuss what is taking place in the system hardware as each event in the operation occurs. This information is a review of the material discussed in detail in Chap. 3. The sequence of events for a RAM read is as follows:

1. Address lines A1–A23 equal the address from which data will be read.

At this point, the system address decoding will occur that will permit the correct address space to become enabled.

2. The 68000 asserts the $\overline{\text{AS}}$ control line.
3. R/$\overline{\text{W}}$ control line is set to a logical 1. This is an indication of a memory READ operation.
4. The 68000 asserts $\overline{\text{UDS}}$, $\overline{\text{LDS}}$, or both control lines.

As the $\overline{\text{UDS}}$ and/or $\overline{\text{LDS}}$ control lines become asserted, several events occur simultanously in the system. These are:

a. The CPU bidirectional buffers are enabled in the correct direction.
b. RAM data is enabled onto the system data bus.

    c. The $\overline{\text{DTACK}}$ input to the 68000 is set to a logical 0, via the external system hardware.

5. Next, the 68000 unasserts the $\overline{\text{UDS}}$, $\overline{\text{LDS}}$, and $\overline{\text{AS}}$ control lines. At this time, the logical condition of the system data bus is strobed into the 68000.

THE HARDWARE EVENT IS NOW COMPLETE

7-3: TROUBLESHOOTING A STATIC RAM READ OPERATION

Using the sequence of events for a RAM READ operation given in Section 7-2, let us examine how to verify each event electrically. As we proceed in the discussion, we will show how the circuit diagram of Fig. 7-1 electrically responds to each step in the sequence.

The first event to occur in the electrical sequence of events is:

ADDRESS LINES A23–A1 ARE SET TO THE MEMORY READ ADDRESS.

This hardware event can be simulated quite easily using the SST. It is exactly what we did when troubleshooting a ROM READ operation. The only difference will be that the address lines will be set to the memory space for system RAM.

In Fig. 7-1, we see that the address space for system RAM is 03000–03FFF in hexadecimal. We will use the address space for 03000–037FF only. To ensure that the address decoding is done correctly, we set the address switches A23–A1 on the SST to 03000.

The address lines BA15–BA12 are input to the 74LS42 BCD to decimal decoder, IC1 (see Fig. 7-1). With the SST address lines set as described, BA12 and BA13 will be a logical 1, BA14 and BA15 will be a logical 0. If these inputs are correct to the 74LS42, then output pin 4 of IC1 will be a logical 0.

We can verify the static condition of output pin 4 of IC1 using a logic probe. If output pin 4 is not a logical 0, then the inputs to the device can be statically checked to verify that they are logically correct. In general, one can troubleshoot the static system and determine the malfunction. It is a typical digital troubleshooting problem at this time, and all standard digital troubleshooting techniques can be employed.

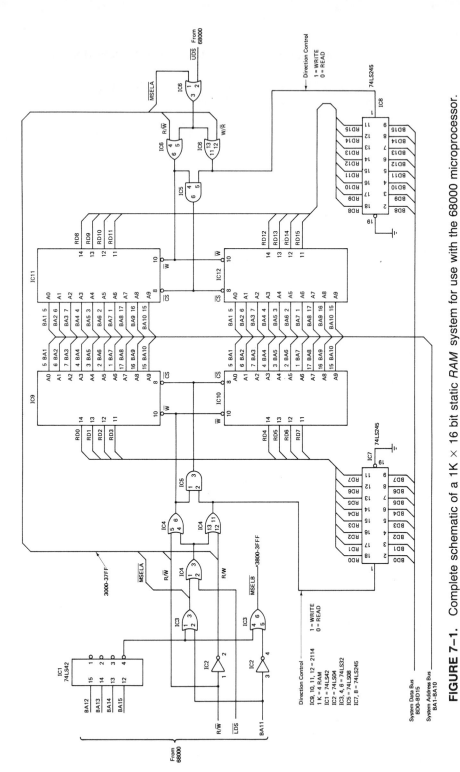

FIGURE 7-1. Complete schematic of a 1K × 16 bit static *RAM* system for use with the 68000 microprocessor.

134

Let us assume that the output pin 4 of IC1 was at the correct logical level. We determine next if all of the parallel address lines, BA1–BA10 to the system RAM, are capable of switching from a logical 0 to a logical 1 under the control of the CPU. This can be accomplished using the following procedure:

1. Set address switches A1–A10 on the SST to the logical 0 position.
2. Set address switch A1 to a logical 1 position.
3. With a logic probe, electrically verify that pin 5 of IC9, IC10, IC11, and IC12 of Fig. 7-1 are a logical 1.
4. With a logic probe electrically verify that all other address inputs to IC9, IC10, IC11, and IC12 are a logical 0.
5. If steps 3 and 4 verify electrically, then we may be certain that address line BA1 can switch between a logical 1 and a logical 0, under the control of the 68000. Further, it has been ensured that the switching of the address lines will occur in a mutually exclusive fashion—that is, no two address lines are shorted together.
6. Set address switch A1 to the logical 0 position.
7. Repeat steps 2, 3, 4, 5, and 6 for the remaining address lines A2–A10.
8. By the end of this sequence, it has been electrically verified that the address path from the 68000 to RAM is valid.

The next hardware event to occur in the RAM READ sequence of events is:

$$\overline{\text{AS}} \text{ IS SET TO A LOGICAL 0.}$$

In the system we are discussing, the $\overline{\text{AS}}$ output will have no effect on the RAM READ operation. It can be verified that the $\overline{\text{AS}}$ output will switch by using a logic probe and monitoring the $\overline{\text{AS}}$ output line on the 68000 device socket.

The next event to occur is:

$$\text{R}/\overline{\text{W}} \text{ IS SET TO A LOGICAL 1.}$$

Figure 7-1 shows that the $\text{R}/\overline{\text{W}}$ line is connected to IC2 pin 1, IC4 pin 5, and IC6 pin 4. The $\text{R}/\overline{\text{W}}$ line is inverted with IC2 and then input to IC4 pin 12 and IC6 pin 12.

At this time, it can be verified that a logical 1 exists on IC2 pin 1, IC4 pin 5, and IC6 pin 4. This logical 1 will disable the OR gates of IC4 and IC6. These OR gates are used in the RAM WRITE operation.

IC4 pin 12 and IC6 pin 12 will have a logical 0 input. This logical 0 is the output from IC2 pin 2. These conditions can be verified by use of a logic probe. What we have done in the preceding checks is to determine if each signal that is logically controlled by the R/$\overline{\text{W}}$ line will switch between a logical 1 and a logical 0. The SST will provide the means for stimulating only a single output line of the 68000 at a time. In this instance, it is the R/$\overline{\text{W}}$ line. As the single line is stimulated, the troubleshooter can concentrate efforts on a specific hardware section of the complete system.

With the R/$\overline{\text{W}}$ line at a logical 1 level and the system address lines at the correct address space, IC4 pin 1 and IC6 pin 1 of Fig. 7-1 will be a logical 0. This may be verified using a logic probe.

The next event to occur in the RAM READ sequence is:

$\overline{\text{UDS}}$, $\overline{\text{LDS}}$, OR BOTH ARE ASSERTED TO A LOGICAL 0.

Several electrical events will now occur. We will examine and verify each event, one at a time.

First, IC4 pin 3 and IC6 pin 3 are set to a logical 0. Notice that IC4 pin 3 is set to a logical 0 under the control of the $\overline{\text{LDS}}$ signal and IC6 pin 3 is set to a logical 0 under the control of the $\overline{\text{UDS}}$ signal.

Pins 2 and 5 of IC5, 74LS08, become a logical 0. With these inputs a logical 0, output pins 3 and 6 are a logical 0. This will assert the $\overline{\text{CS}}$ inputs to IC9, IC10, IC11, and IC12. These logical conditions can be verified using a logic probe. We are ensuring that the memory devices can become enabled at the correct time.

Second, the memory data buffers, IC7 and IC8, have their direction control line set to the logical level that will place memory data onto the system data bus. This means that pins 1 of both IC7 and IC8, 74LS245s, are set to a logical 0.

Data at the RAM memory outputs is logically in control of the system data bus lines BD0–BD15. These data outputs will visually show up on the LEDs of the SST. It should be noted that one does not know what should be the logical conditions of the RAM data output. This is because we have not written any data to the RAM. Whatever data was present in the RAM prior to the READ operation will be the data that is read at the SST LEDs by the user.

Third, the $\overline{\text{DTACK}}$ input to the 68000 will be set to a logical 0 under the control of the external hardware. This event can be verified by monitoring the $\overline{\text{DTACK}}$ input pin 10 on the 68000 socket.

The final event to occur in the RAM READ sequence of events is:

$$\overline{\text{UDS}}, \overline{\text{LDS}} \text{ AND } \overline{\text{AS}} \text{ ARE SET TO A LOGICAL 1 LEVEL.}$$

The $\overline{\text{CS}}$ input to the 2114 memory chips is now set to a logical 1. The memory data buffers have the direction control lines set to a logical 1. This is input pin 1 on IC7 and IC8. With the unassertion of $\overline{\text{LDS}}$ and $\overline{\text{UDS}}$, the sequence of events is complete.

It should be noted that only the lower byte or the upper byte of RAM could have been enabled onto the system data bus. This action is controlled by the assertion of the $\overline{\text{UDS}}$ for the upper data byte and $\overline{\text{LDS}}$ for the lower data byte. Also note that all of the hardware operations performed by the 68000 SST were static.

The electrical operation of all interface circuits may be verified using SST techniques. The system does not have to be executing a program. While it is true that the memory is not executing at system speed, the memory will have to operate at static speed before it will operate at system speed.

In this section, we did not verify all memory locations of the system RAM. This would take a very long time to accomplish using only the manual SST. The main point in using SST is to verify that path from the RAM to the CPU. If this path is operational, then we can use the CPU to help in the troubleshooting process. This will be accomplished using software memory diagnostics. (A memory diagnostic is given in Chap. 9.)

Next, we will show how the SST can be used to verify the write section of the RAM hardware path. In that discussion, we will actually write data to either the upper byte, lower byte, or both using the 68000 SST. After the data is written, a READ sequence of events will be performed to verify that the WRITE operation was successful.

7-4: SEQUENCE OF EVENTS FOR A MEMORY WRITE OPERATION

The following is the electrical sequence of events that will occur when the 68000 writes data to RAM.

1. First, A23–A1 are set to the address where data will be stored.
2. $\overline{\text{AS}}$ is asserted by the 68000. This signal may or may not be used by the hardware of a particular system.

3. R/$\overline{\text{W}}$ is set to a logical 0. This is an electrical indication that a WRITE operation will occur.

4. The 68000 will output data to be written on the data lines D0–D15.

5. $\overline{\text{LDS}}$ or $\overline{\text{UDS}}$ control lines are asserted. $\overline{\text{LDS}}$ will write data to the lower byte of memory and $\overline{\text{UDS}}$ will write data to the upper byte of memory.

6. Next, the external hardware will respond with the $\overline{\text{DTACK}}$ signal to be input to the 68000.

7. Finally, the 68000 will unassert the $\overline{\text{LDS}}$ or $\overline{\text{UDS}}$ control lines.

AT THIS TIME, THE MEMORY WRITE OPERATION IS COMPLETE.

7-5: TROUBLESHOOTING A MEMORY WRITE OPERATION

In this section, we will discuss how to verify the hardware response to the sequence of events given in Section 7-4.

ADDRESS LINES A1–A23 ARE SET TO THE CORRECT ADDRESS OF MEM.

First, the address lines A1–A23 are set to the correct memory address. We can simulate the hardware action by setting the address switches on the SST to 003000 base 16.

We discussed the details of how the address lines are decoded when showing how to read data from the memory. Therefore, we will not spend time on the address decoding for a memory WRITE operation. Our discussion will start by assuming that the address has been output and is decoded properly.

$\overline{\text{AS}}$ IS ASSERTED TO A LOGICAL 0.

The 68000 will now assert the $\overline{\text{AS}}$ control signal to a logical 0. In our memory circuit, the $\overline{\text{AS}}$ control line is not used. The electrical operation of the $\overline{\text{AS}}$ control line can be verified by use of a logic probe to monitor the $\overline{\text{AS}}$ output and by toggling the $\overline{\text{AS}}$ switch on the SST.

R/W IS SET TO A LOGICAL 0.

Referring to Fig. 7-1, we see that the R/W is input to IC4 pin 5 and IC6 pin 4. These two pins may be verified using a logic probe. If either of these two lines fail to verify, then the fault can be traced using static, digital troubleshooting techniques.

68000 WILL OUTPUT DATA ON D15–D0.

Next, CPU will output the data to write to the memory on the system data bus. The origin of the data is the CPU data output pins. Figure 7-2 shows the block diagram of the path for data from the CPU data output pins to the data buffers, and finally to the memory data input lines. The data buffers shown in Fig. 7-1 are 74LS245s. Input pins 1 of both IC7 and IC8 are a logical 1. This will enable the bidirectional data buffers to place data from the CPU data bus to the memory data input pins.

It can be easily verified that the data lines from the CPU data output pins are electrically reaching the input lines to the 74LS245s, IC7 and IC8 by following a four-step procedure:

1. Set all the data switches on the SST to a logical 0 position.
2. Set the data switch on the SST labeled "D0" to the logical 1 position.
3. Using a logical probe, verify that the input pin 2 of IC7 of Fig. 7-1 is a logical 1.
4. Repeat steps 2 and 3 for the remaining data lines D1–D15.

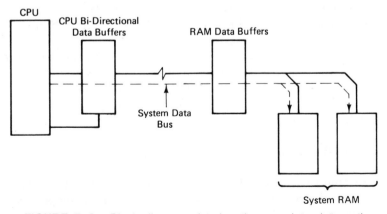

FIGURE 7–2. Block diagram showing the complete data path from the 68000 to the system *RAM* chips.

If at any time the data inputs to the 74LS245s fail to respond correctly, then leave the system set up in the static condition and concentrate on the single digital line that is malfunctioning. Using SST techniques, no other system signal line need be used—that is, focus all efforts on troubleshooting a single digital line that is not responding correctly. Again, note that this is a standard digital troubleshooting problem. The problem has been reduced to this via the use of the SST.

Let us assume that the data inputs to the 75LS245's, IC7 and IC8 of Fig. 7-1, are electrically valid. The hardware path from the CPU through the CPU bidirectional buffers to the bidirectional buffers of the static RAM is operational.

We must now verify that the data at the output of the 74LS245's is being input to the memory. This can be accomplished by repeating the procedure for checking the inputs to the 74LS245's just outlined. The difference is that now the data input lines to the system RAM, rather than the inputs to the 74LS245's, must be monitored.

We will assume that this data path is correct. The next hardware event to occur in the memory WRITE operation is the CPU will:

68000 ASSERTS THE $\overline{\text{UDS}}$ OR $\overline{\text{LDS}}$.

At this time, the data at the memory data input lines will be written to the memory. The $\overline{\text{CS}}$ inputs, pin 8, of the 2114 RAMs and the $\overline{\text{WE}}$ inputs, pin 10, will be a logical 0. This can be verified this using a logic probe. It should be noted in Fig. 7-1 that the $\overline{\text{UDS}}$ control line will assert the $\overline{\text{WE}}$ and $\overline{\text{CS}}$ inputs to 2114 devices IC11 and IC12. The $\overline{\text{LDS}}$ control line will assert the $\overline{\text{WE}}$ and $\overline{\text{CS}}$ inputs to the 2114 devices IC9 and IC10.

The 68000 will assert one or both of these control lines based on the software instruction being executed. As a system hardware troubleshooter, you must ensure that when either of these control lines are asserted, the $\overline{\text{WE}}$ and $\overline{\text{CS}}$ of the proper memory devices is asserted.

$\overline{\text{DTACK}}$ IS ASSERTED BY EXTERNAL HARDWARE.

At this time, the external hardware will assert the $\overline{\text{DTACK}}$ input to the 68000. Figure 7-3 shows how this is accomplished in this system.

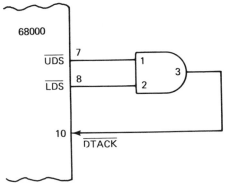

FIGURE 7–3. Schematic diagram showing how the $\overline{DTACK}$ input signal will become asserted.

$\overline{UDS}$ AND $\overline{LDS}$ ARE UNASSERTED BY THE 68000.

The final event to occur in the memory WRITE operation is the $\overline{UDS}$ and the $\overline{LDS}$ are set to the logical 1 position by the CPU. Now, the hardware event is complete. The data that was placed on the system data bus will be written into the RAM space selected by the address combination set on the SST address switches.

We have no way of knowing if the WRITE operation was successful. That is, we have determined that all of the physical lines involved in the hardware operation can switch at the correct time. However, we have not yet determined if the RAM devices electrically accepted and latched the data internally.

This can be electrically verified by performing the sequence of electrical events for a memory READ operation at the same address space where we have just written data. By doing this, known data can be input to the RAM and then read back using the SST. This action will ensure that all address decoding, data lines, and control lines are electrically capable of switching under the control of the CPU.

What we have done is to determine that all of the hardware paths for RAM communication in the system are valid. If a manual SST were being used, it would take quite a long time to determine if all of the available memory space were operational. What is needed is a software diagnostic that will test the memory at system speed. Be aware that memory diagnostics are only effective if the CPU can read data from ROM. The SST is the easiest and most straightforward tool to get the system ROM operational.

The first step in troubleshooting a malfunctioning RAM memory system is to verify that all of the hardware paths are electrically valid. From this point, a memory test may be run to find any cells of the memory that are not functional. As a system troubleshooter, the sequence might be to run the memory test first to determine if any of the memory locations can be written to and read from. Based on the results of the software diagnostic, you can focus in on the problem area using SST.

A memory diagnostic will be shown and discussed in Chap. 9.

7-6: CHAPTER SUMMARY

In this chapter, we have discussed how to use the SST in verifying the operation of system memory in a 68000 microprocessor system. We have also discussed the details of how typical system hardware responds in a static fashion to a stimulus originating at the CPU.

This was a general concept that is often overlooked in the troubleshooting aspect of microprocessor systems. The static RAM READ and WRITE operations are truely static in all respects. We made use of this fact and SST to verify all of the hardware that is involved in the memory READ and WRITE operations.

In the next chapter, we will show how SST and static operation of a microprocessor system can be used very effectively to troubleshoot the hardware of input and output operations.

CHAPTER **8**

TROUBLESHOOTING AN INPUT OR OUTPUT OPERATION

In this chapter, we will discuss how to approach the problem of troubleshooting a defective input or output device in a 68000 microprocessor system. The input and output devices we will use are the same ones that are presented in Chap. 3. The discussion of troubleshooting the I/O ports will be general enough to be of value for almost any type of input and output operation. However, we will be specific in the procedures so that you may see exactly how to apply the troubleshooting techniques.

The discussion will start with an overview of the I/O ports that were presented in Chap. 3. Following the overview of the input and output ports we will present the sequence of electrical events that the 68000 will execute whenever an I/O operation occurs. These events were first given in Chap. 3 and are reviewed here. Finally, after you understand how the I/O devices operate by performing a sequence of electrical events, we will show how to verify electrical operation using Static Stimulus Testing. During this discussion, you will be made aware of exactly how SST techniques can enable the system troubleshooter to isolate hardware faults associated with input and output devices.

Do not be misled into thinking that, because we are showing how to use SST with discrete input and output ports, the technique is valid only for similarly designed ports. Nothing could be further from the truth: I/O ports designed using LSI devices such as PIO, PIA, or SIOs, or virtually any LSI device, can be electrically verified using SST. The procedures are similar to the ones we will show in this chapter.

The schematics and ports presented were chosen simply as the medium for the information transfer. These input and output ports are general enough to allow SST techniques and procedures to be explained without the reader having to understand and learn how any particular LSI device operates.

8-1: OVERVIEW OF THE INPUT AND OUTPUT PORTS

In the following section, we will discuss how the input and output circuits presented in Chap. 3 operate. It is essential to know how the circuit operates before making an attempt to troubleshoot it. You must know what should be there, otherwise measurements made and data acquired will tell you nothing.

Figure 8-1 shows a block diagram of the input and output circuits. We see in Fig. 8-1 that external digital signals are input to the input block of the circuit. These external digital signals are outputs from instruments, or devices, that the microprocessor system is communicating with. The input circuit is physically capable of accepting data from 16 external lines.

The output section of the circuit is capable of outputting up to 16 lines of external information. These output lines can be used to control external instruments connected to the circuit.

The address decoding block shown in Fig. 8-1 will logically select the I/O port from the entire address space available in a 68000 system. Notice that all addresses A1–A23 are input to the address decoding block of Fig. 8-1.

Control signal inputs to Fig. 8-1 are the R/$\overline{\text{W}}$, $\overline{\text{UDS}}$, and $\overline{\text{LDS}}$ lines from the 68000 CPU. We will see later that when the R/$\overline{\text{W}}$ is a

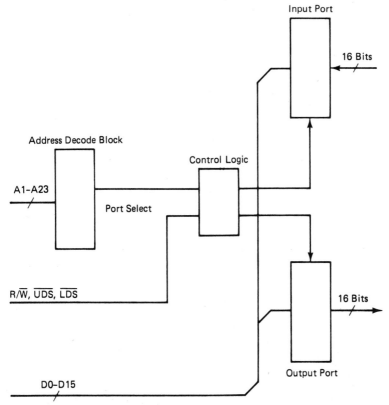

FIGURE 8–1. Block diagram of a general 16-bit input and output port for use with the 68000 *CPU.*

logical 1 and $\overline{\text{UDS}}$ or $\overline{\text{LDS}}$ control lines are a logical 0, the data from the input port is placed on the system data bus.

Data outputs from the input port block are sent to the system data bus via a bus buffer. When the R/$\overline{\text{W}}$ is a logical 0 and the $\overline{\text{UDS}}$ or $\overline{\text{LDS}}$ is a logical 0, the data on the system data bus will be written to the output port block shown in Fig. 8-1.

8-2: SEQUENCE OF EVENTS FOR READING DATA FROM AN INPUT PORT

Let us now show the sequence of events for an input READ operation using the 68000 CPU. This sequence is exactly the same as we presented in Chap. 3. If you do not understand why the sequence is given in the order shown, please refer back to Chap. 3 for a complete discussion of this sequence.

After the sequence of events is given, we will show how to verify the hardware response to the sequence using SST.

1. First, the system address bus outputs the port address to read data from. All system address lines are used in the decoding of the input port. This is true for the input port that we will present. However, it need not be true in all 68000 microprocessor systems. Recall that the I/O space in the 68000 is memory-mapped.

2. Next, the CPU will assert the $\overline{AS}$ control line.

The address is now decoded by the input port and the port select line is generated. If an address latch is used, the system address will remain stable until another $\overline{AS}$ signal is asserted to the system by the 68000.

3. Next, the R/$\overline{W}$ control line from the CPU will go to a logical 1. This signal will electrically inform the 68000 system that a READ operation will occur.

4. Fourth, the $\overline{UDS}$, $\overline{LDS}$, or both are asserted to a logical 0, under the control of the 68000.

Input port data is now placed on the system data bus. The origin of the data is the input port, and the destination for the data is the 68000 CPU input pins.

5. When the $\overline{UDS}$ or $\overline{LDS}$ control signals are a logical 0, the input port will respond and assert the $\overline{DTACK}$ input to the 68000. This indicates that the external hardware is electrically prepared to resume normal execution.

6. The final event to occur in the input READ operation is that $\overline{UDS}$, $\overline{LDS}$, and AS are set to a logical 1 under the control of the 68000.

On the rising edge of a $\overline{UDS}$ or $\overline{LDS}$ control signal, the logical conditions of the system data bus are strobed into an internal register on the 68000.

THE HARDWARE EVENT IS NOW COMPLETE.

8-3:   HARDWARE RESPONSE TO THE SEQUENCE OF EVENTS

Now, let us go through the sequence of events just given and examine exactly how the hardware will respond to each event. As we describe the hardware operation, you will see exactly how SST can be used to verify proper electrical operation. As the discussion proceeds, try to relate the hardware operation to another system of personal interest.

Figure 8-2b shows the hardware schematic for the actual input port. We will center our discussion around the logic of this circuit.

THE ADDRESS IS OUTPUT FROM THE 68000.

As you will remember, the first electrical event to occur in the input READ operation is the address lines A1–A23 will output the correct input port address for reading data. Let us review how the address lines are decoded. The logic for decoding the address lines is shown in Fig. 8-2a.

In Fig. 8-2a, the address lines A1–A22 are input to the 74LS30, IC1, IC2, and IC3. Output pins 8 of IC1 and IC2 are input to IC4. Output pin 3 of IC4 and output pin 8 of IC3 are input to pins 4 and 5 of IC4. When the address inputs A1–A22 = 7FFFFF or 7FFFFE, output pin 6 of IC4 is a logical 0. This output is a logical 0 only at these two unique system addresses.

We can verify the hardware operation of each device output in Fig. 8-2a by placing the correct logical combination on the address inputs A1–A22. This can be accomplished using the SST. For example, suppose we wished to verify that IC1 output pin 8 will become asserted, logical 0, when it is electrically supposed to. Using the SST, we set the address lines A1–A8 equal to logical 1.

This will place a logical 1 on all input pins of IC1. We can verify the logical conditions of these inputs by using a logic probe. The output pin 8 of IC1 will now be a logical 0. This logical condition can be verified using a logic probe. Using the information given thus far, the hardware operation of IC2 and IC3 of Fig. 8-2a can be verified.

Let us assume that output pin 8 of all the 74LS30's shown in Fig. 8-2a are set to a logical 0 using the SST as the input stimulus to the gates. Now the output pin 3 of IC4 will be a logical 0. Pins 1 and 2 of IC4 can be verified using a logic probe. With pins 1 and 2 becoming a logical 0, the output pin 3 of IC4 will become a logical 0.

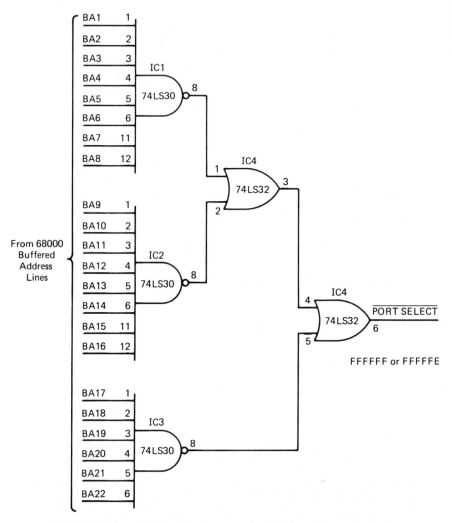

FIGURE 8–2a.   Schematic diagram showing how the port select signal can be generated with hardware. The port will respond to address FFFFFF or FFFFFE.

With pin 3 at a logical 0 level, input pin 4 of IC4 will be set to a logical 0. Pin 5 of IC4 will be a logical 0, due to output pin 8 of IC3 being equal to a logical 0.

As both input pins 4 and 5 of IC4 become a logical 0, output pin 6 is set to a logical 0. The entire operation of decoding the input port address is a static, combinational logical operation. Each level of decoding can be verified using SST as the input stimulus and a logic probe of dc measurement tool to verify logic operation.

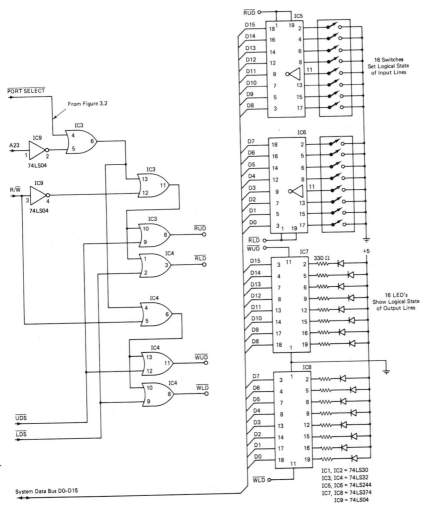

FIGURE 8–2b. Schematic diagram of the input port and output port control and latch circuits.

$\overline{AS}$ IS SET TO A LOGICAL 0.

The next step in the sequence of events for an input READ operation is the $\overline{AS}$ output line from the 68000 is set to a logical 0. This electrical event will latch the address output if an address latch is used in the system. If an address latch is not used in the system, then the $\overline{AS}$ output may synchronize certain 68000 inputs from the external hardware. An example of this is the VPA input that is used for communication with external 6800-type peripheral devices. For our discussion, the $\overline{AS}$ output of the 68000 is not used here, and in some systems $\overline{AS}$ may not have any electrical effect on the external hardware.

R/$\overline{W}$ IS SET TO A LOGICAL 1.

The next event to occur in the electrical sequence of events is the R/W output from the 68000 is set to a logical 1. In this way the external hardware is informed that a READ operation will occur during the CPU execution cycle. In Fig. 8-2b, we see that the R/$\overline{W}$ output is inverted and input to IC3 pin 12. Input pin 12 of IC3 is a logical 0 if, and only if, the R/$\overline{W}$ is a logical 1.

Pin 13 of IC3 in Fig. 8-2b is a logical 0 when the port address is equal to 7FFFFF or 7FFFFE and address line A23 is a logical 1. This will be address FFFFFE or FFFFFF and is the logical condition of the address bus selecting the input port. When address line A23 is a logical 1, the system is performing I/O operations. This is determined by the system design. In a memory-mapped I/O system, a certain portion of the available memory space is reserved for I/O.

With input pins 12 and 13 of IC3 a logical 0, output pin 11 is a logical 0. Pin 11 of IC3 is connected to input pins 10 and 1 of IC3. These input pins will enable the OR gates with output pins 8 and 3. Output pins 3 and 8 will not be a logical 0 at this time.

Again, we note that all of the preceding operations in the 68000 system hardware are static. The operations can be verified using SST and standard digital troubleshooting techniques. The troubleshooter may concentrate efforts on only one signal in the total system at any given time. Furthermore, the signal is static. This will help enormously when isolating a malfunction on a particular signal line.

$\overline{UDS}$, $\overline{LDS}$ OR BOTH ARE SET TO A LOGICAL 0.

Next, the $\overline{UDS}$ or $\overline{LDS}$ control line from the CPU will become asserted. We can simulate this event by placing the $\overline{UDS}$ or $\overline{LDS}$ switch on the SST into the logical 0 position.

$\overline{UDS}$ output of the input port circuit of Fig. 8-2b is connected to input pin 9 of the 74LS32 IC3. With both input pins 9 and 10 of IC3 at a logical 0 level, output pin 8 will be a logical 0. The $\overline{LDS}$ output from the 68000 is connected to input pin 2 of IC4, shown in Fig. 8-2b. With input pins 2 and 1 at a logical 0 level, output pin 3 of IC4 will be a logical 0.

The outputs of IC5 and IC6 of the 74LS244's are now logically connected to the system data bus. This is due to the input pins 1 and 19 of IC 5 and IC6 ($\overline{\text{RUD}}$ and $\overline{\text{RLD}}$) being asserted to a logical 0 level. These are the enable input lines for the 74LS244's.

Let us review exactly in what state the input circuit is set up.

1. The address is fully decoded; port is selected.
2. A23 is a logical 1, indicating an I/O operation.
3. R/$\overline{\text{W}}$ is a logical 1.
4. $\overline{\text{UDS}}$ and $\overline{\text{LDS}}$ are both a logical 0.

The input data from an external device is, at this point, logically in control of the system data bus. For our system, we see that the external inputs, pins 17, 15, 13, 11, 2, 4, 6 and 8 of IC5 and IC6 of Fig. 8-2b are in control of the system data bus. This is because IC5 and IC6 are enabled via $\overline{\text{RUD}}$ and $\overline{\text{RLD}}$, respectively.

At the SST data LEDs, we can verify visually that the logical conditions that exist on the input lines to IC5 and IC6 are physically reaching the CPU data input pins. The data seen at the LEDs on the SST will be dependent on the data present at the data input pins of IC5 and IC6. (See Fig. 8-3.)

If we are interested in verifying the operation of IC5 or IC6 with no external device connected, we can force data at the input of IC5 or IC6 and examine the response at the SST LEDs. For example, with none of the external switches connected to IC5 or IC6 data input lines, all lines will be a logical 1. This is due to the floating input. A floating input on a TTL device is electrically treated as a logical 1.

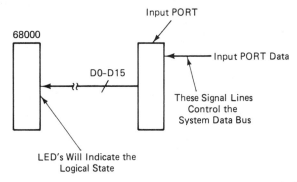

FIGURE 8-3. Block diagram showing how the external signals connected to the input port will control the logical state of the data bus. These external signals will be the logical inputs to the 68000 during an input operation.

With the system statically set in the preceding condition, all of the LEDs on the SST will indicate a logical 1 on each line of the system data bus. The external input pins can be grounded one at a time via the external switch provided. As each pin is grounded, the corresponding LED on the SST will reflect the logical 0. (See Fig. 8-4 for a block diagram representation of exactly what is occurring in the system.)

This type of verification is exactly what we used for verifying the memory data path. Further, this verification may be performed on any of the existing input ports of a system, the only difference being that the address lines will change to enable a different input port.

In a typical system in use in industry, there probably will not be external switches neatly connected to the input port. The data input lines may come from many different transducers or from monitor points in the control loop. If this is the case, then the input line can be examined with a logic probe to determine what the data shown on the SST LEDs should be.

$\overline{\text{DTACK}}$ INPUT TO THE 68000 IS SET TO A LOGICAL 0.

When $\overline{\text{UDS}}$ or $\overline{\text{LDS}}$ are asserted to the logical 0 state by the 68000, the $\overline{\text{DTACK}}$ input must also be asserted to a logical 0. This input must be a logical 0 before the 68000 will electrically proceed in the hardware operation. This input signal is used to inform the 68000 that the external hardware device is ready to proceed.

Figure 8-5 shows how the $\overline{\text{DTACK}}$ input to the 68000 is asserted (as discussed in Chaps. 6 and 7). If the $\overline{\text{DTACK}}$ input is

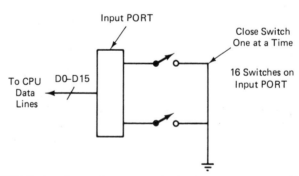

FIGURE 8–4.   General concept of stimulating one external input signal at a time and monitoring the result on the 68000 *SST LEDs*. In the input port we are using, this is easy to do because of the 16 *SPST* switches connected as input data.

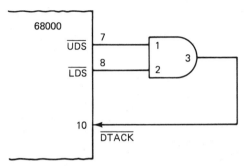

FIGURE 8–5. Schematic diagram showing how the *DTACK* input to the 68000 is asserted via the external hardware. Note, if this were an I/O operation with a 6800 type of external device, the *DTACK* input must be held at a logical 1. This circuit would not do the job.

asserted in a different manner on another system, the electrical response by the CPU would be the same. No matter how the external hardware is designed to assert the $\overline{\text{DTACK}}$ input to the 68000, the signal would go to a logical 0 after the $\overline{\text{UDS}}$ or $\overline{\text{LDS}}$ outputs have become asserted.

An LED in the 68000 SST will visually show the logical level of the $\overline{\text{DTACK}}$ input line. If the $\overline{\text{DTACK}}$ input is not asserted at this time, leave the system set up statically and determine the cause. Again, now the problem is reduced to a familiar digital troubleshooting one of finding out why a particular digital signal failed to respond to a given stimulus. Let us assume that the $\overline{\text{DTACK}}$ input to the 68000 responded as it should.

$\overline{\text{UDS}}$, $\overline{\text{LDS}}$, AND $\overline{\text{AS}}$ ARE SET TO A LOGICAL 1.

The final event in the input READ operation is the $\overline{\text{UDS}}$, $\overline{\text{LDS}}$, and $\overline{\text{AS}}$ control lines from the CPU will become unasserted. This can be simulated by placing the corresponding SST switches to the logical 1 position. With the SST switches in this condition, the $\overline{\text{RUD}}$ or the $\overline{\text{RLD}}$ line in the circuit of Fig. 8-2b will be a logical 1. Data from the selected input port are removed from the system data bus.

THE HARDWARE EVENT IS COMPLETE.

We have just examined and electrically verified the hardware response of the input READ operation using the SST. This type of hardware verification is easy to perform on most microprocessor systems. The main focus in the troubleshooting is to ensure that the hardware path for data, address, and control are logically valid. Notice that each path is independent and completely static in operation.

Most electrical verification is concerned with the operation of combinational logic circuits. This verification is easy to do when an SST type of instrument and a logic probe are used. If the hardware fails to respond correctly, the system may be "frozen" in the failed state to locate the malfunction.

With the system in a failed state, the path of the failed signal can be traced and standard digital troubleshooting techniques can be applied to finding the source of trouble. The system need not be in a dynamic environment for one to solve most hardware troubleshooting problems.

8-4: TROUBLESHOOTING AN OUTPUT OPERATION

In the remaining sections of this text, we will discuss how to verify electrically the hardware used in an output operation. This type of system debugging is useful when interfacing, or troubleshooting, a defective output port in a microprocessor system. To show how SST can be used in troubleshooting output operations, we will make use of the output port circuit discussed in Chap. 3.

The output port is 16 bits wide and designed to fit into the 68000 system architecture. The port is designed using discrete TTL devices and is similar in concept to the input port discussed previously.

To start the discussion, an overview of the output port block diagram will be given. Next we will review the sequence of events that occurs each time the 68000 writes data to an output port. Following this review, it will be shown how to verify the system hardware at each step in the sequence. Again, we state that this type of hardware verification may be applied to most 68000 microprocessor systems. This particular output port was chosen to instruct and give a real example of using SST techniques.

Figure 8-6 shows a block diagram of the output port circuit. In Fig. 8-6, there are 16 physical output lines shown. The output port is capable of latching 16 bits of data in a parallel fashion from the CPU and outputting the 16 bits of data to an external instrument.

The source of data is the CPU data output pins. Data from the CPU is input to all output ports in the system. Only the output port

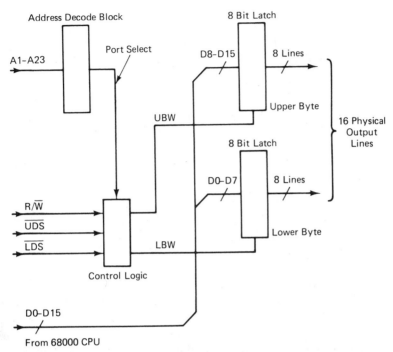

FIGURE 8–6. Block diagram showing the major hardware blocks of a general 16-bit output port for use with the 68000.

that is decoded by the address bus will use the data on the system data bus lines.

Address inputs to the output circuit are A1–A23. These are the same address inputs that were used for the input port circuit. The *address decoding block* of Fig. 8-6 is the section of hardware the output port uses to enable the circuit logically.

The strobing of data at the output port is accomplished by the *control logic block* shown in Fig. 8-6. Inputs to the control block are R/W̄, ŪDS, L̄DS, and the port select line from the address decoding block. Outputs from the control logic block are W̄ŪD and W̄LD. These two signals will strobe the data for the upper byte, lower byte, or both, at the correct time in the output transfer cycle.

8-5: SEQUENCE OF EVENTS FOR AN OUTPUT WRITE OPERATION

With this introduction to the output port circuit, let us review the sequence of events for an output WRITE operation. After this review, we will show exactly how the microprocessor hardware responds and how to verify electrically each step in the sequence.

1. First, the address lines A1–A23 will output the port address where data will be written.

At this time, the address decoders in the microprocessor system will decode the port address for the selected output port.

2. Next, the CPU will assert the $\overline{\text{AS}}$ control line. This is the hardware signal that indicates to the system that the CPU is outputting valid address data on A1–A23.
3. The CPU will set the R/$\overline{\text{W}}$ control line to a logical 0, indicating that a WRITE operation will occur.
4. The CPU outputs the data to be written to the address output port on the system data bus.
5. Next, the CPU asserts the $\overline{\text{UDS}}$, $\overline{\text{LDS}}$, or both control lines. These are the timed control signals that will start the data transfer at the selected output port.
6. The $\overline{\text{DTACK}}$ input is asserted via the external hardware. This is an electrical indication that the system hardware is ready to proceed in the transfer.
7. Finally, the CPU will unassert the $\overline{\text{UDS}}$, $\overline{\text{LDS}}$, and $\overline{\text{AS}}$ control lines.

THE HARDWARE TRANSFER IS NOW COMPLETE.

8-6: VERIFYING THE HARDWARE RESPONSE TO THE SEQUENCE OF EVENTS

Let us now use the sequence of events just given and the SST to verify the hardware response. Keep in mind that the hardware response may be unique for each system, but the sequence of events will remain constant. It could be helpful to understanding if you were to examine another system of hardware and think through the hardware response of that system.

The first step in the sequence of events is:

ADDRESS IS OUTPUT ON THE ADDRESS LINES.

The address decoding for the port circuit is exactly the same as for the input port. You are asked to refer to the section of the chapter dealing with the address decoding for the input port to see exactly how this function may be verified using SST.

$\overline{AS}$ IS SET TO A LOGICAL 0.

The 68000 will now set the $\overline{AS}$ control line to a logical 0. In some systems, this signal is not used. In other systems, the $\overline{AS}$ control line will synchronize some of the external transfers. An example is the $\overline{VPA}$ input to the 68000. This input electrically informs the CPU that a 6800-type peripheral device will be communicated with.

R/$\overline{W}$ OUTPUT IS SET TO A LOGICAL 0.

When the R/$\overline{W}$ control line from the 68000 is set to a logical 0, it is an indication to the external hardware that a WRITE operation will occur. In Fig. 8-2b, we see that the R/$\overline{W}$ output is connected to pin 5 of IC4. When R/$\overline{W}$ is a logical 0, the OR gate contained in IC4 with pin 6 as the output is enabled.

Input pin 4 of IC4 is the *port select* line. This line will be a logical 0 when the port address is present on the 68000 address bus and the 68000 is electrically communicating with I/O. This same port select line is used for the input and output port select decoding. The 16-bit port is truly an I/O port.

With the system set in the preceding state, all logical conditions exist for proper operation of the output decoding circuit. This circuit may be verified by use of the SST—that is, the address lines and the R/$\overline{W}$ line can be set to the correct logical levels using the SST. Output pin 6 of IC4 may be examined using a logic probe.

Output pin 6 will be a logical 0 when the circuit is operating correctly. If pin 6 is not a logical 0, the decoding circuit may be statically traced back to the source of the stimulus to isolate the malfunction. The source of all stimulus for the circuit is the 68000 or, more precisely, the 68000 SST.

CPU OUTPUTS DATA TO BE WRITTEN TO THE OUTPUT PORT.

Using the SST, we can simulate this function quite easily. To accomplish this, the switches labeled "D0–D15" are set to the data we wish to transfer to the output port latch. For testing purposes, we will transfer a pattern of alternate 1's and 0's. This means that the data word to output on the data bus is either 5555 or AAAA base 16.

Let us output 5555 on the data bus. This will mean that D0, D2, D4, D6, D8, D10, D12, and D14 will be a logical 1. All other data bits will be a logical 0. The data pattern is:

D15   D0
0–1–0–1   0–1–0–1   0–1–0–1   0–1–0–1

With this data pattern set on the SST data switches, the system troubleshooter may verify that the information can electrically reach the data latches IC7 and IC8 shown in Fig. 8-2b. Using a logic probe, the logical condition of each input pin of IC7 and IC8 of the 74LS374 can be verified. If any of the data bits fail to indicate the correct logical level, then the troubleshooter can determine the cause.

Let us assume that all data inputs to the 74LS374 latches of Fig. 8-2b are correct. The next event to occur in the output operation is:

$\overline{\text{UDS}}$ OR $\overline{\text{LDS}}$ CONTROL LINES ARE ASSERTED TO '0'.

We can simulate this operation by setting the $\overline{\text{UDS}}$ or $\overline{\text{LDS}}$ switch on the SST to the logical 0 position. In examining the schematic of Fig. 8-2b, we see that the $\overline{\text{UDS}}$ signal is input to IC4 pin 12. IC4 pin 13 will be a logical 0 due to the $\overline{\text{R/W}}$ being set to a logical 0 by the 68000 and the port select line decoding the correct port address.

With $\overline{\text{UDS}}$ going to a logical 0, the output pin 11 of IC4 is set to a logical 0. This signal is labeled "$\overline{\text{WUD}}$" (Write Upper Data). When this signal is a logical 0, the data strobe to the upper data byte latch, IC7, is set to a logical 0.

When the preceding operation occurs, the data will not be strobed into the latch. The timing diagram for the data transfer with a 68000 microprocessor indicates that data should be transferred on the positive-going edge of the $\overline{\text{UDS}}$ control line. The 74LS374 latch is designed to transfer data on the positive-going edge of the clock input pin 11.

When the $\overline{\text{WUD}}$ signal is set to a logical 1 under the control of the 68000, the data at the input pin of the 74LS374, IC7, will be transferred to the latch output pins.

In Fig. 8-2b, we see that the $\overline{\text{LDS}}$ output from the 68000 is input to pin 9 of IC4. Pin 10 of IC4 is set to a logical 0 at the same time as pin 13 described for the $\overline{\text{UDS}}$ signal. When the $\overline{\text{LDS}}$ is set to a logical 0, the output pin 8 of IC4 is set to a logical 0. This output is labeled "$\overline{\text{WLD}}$" (Write Lower Data). When this line switches from a logical 1 to a logical 0, and back to a logical 1 again, the data on the lower byte of the system data bus is transferred to the 74LS374 IC8 latch outputs.

It can be seen from the individual control of the $\overline{\text{UDS}}$ and $\overline{\text{LDS}}$ lines that either the upper data byte, the lower data byte, or both can be written to the output port by the 68000 during a single output transfer.

The next event to occur in the output operation is:

$\overline{\text{DTACK}}$ INPUT IS ASSERTED BY EXTERNAL HARDWARE.

Figure 8-5 showed how this operation was accomplished in the system. This event can be monitored by an LED on the 68000 SST that is connected to the $\overline{\text{DTACK}}$ input pin. (See Fig. 8-7.) If the $\overline{\text{DTACK}}$ input is not valid at this time, then the malfunction may be traced using static digital troubleshooting techniques. It should be noted that either $\overline{\text{UDS}}$ or $\overline{\text{LDS}}$ must be a logical 0 for the $\overline{\text{DTACK}}$ to be a logical 0, as shown in Fig. 8-5.

The final step in the output operation is:

$\overline{\text{UDS}}$, $\overline{\text{LDS}}$, AND $\overline{\text{AS}}$ CONTROL LINES ARE UNASSERTED VIA THE CPU.

At the time control lines go to a logical 1, the hardware event is complete. The data that was present on the system data bus will have been written to the selected output port. Notice that by using

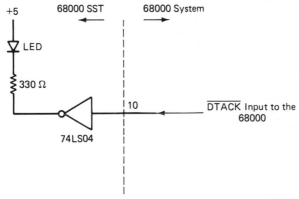

FIGURE 8–7.   Schematic diagram showing how the $\overline{\text{DTACK}}$ input to the 68000 can be visually monitored on the SST.

the SST any data desired can be written to an output port. This means that if an output device requires a certain word to perform a particular function, we can write that word to the output device.

For example, suppose an output device requires a certain word to turn on a motor or a light. That word can be written to the port using the SST. The output device can be controlled in exactly the same way the CPU would be doing if a program were running. In this way, the output receiving hardware of the interface can also be troubleshooted. The output port can be checked to determine if the correct word is being written to the device. After that, the device can be checked to determine if it is responding to the correct word in the appropriate way.

8-7: CHAPTER SUMMARY

In this chapter, we have discussed the sequence of events required for reading and writing data to an I/O port. The discussion centered on the use of the SST. It was shown how to verify each section of system hardware involved in the I/O operation.

The discussions were general enough to allow one to adopt and modify the details to any microprocessor system that has been designed around the 68000 microprocessor. Main points of the discussions were to make you aware of the complete static operation of microprocessor systems. Using SST, you can take advantage of the static nature of microprocessor systems and reduce the troubleshooting problem to a standard digital one.

We did not outline exact procedures in this chapter. Rather, we presented essential details that would allow the reader to understand how to apply SST.

The SST concept of microprocessor troubleshooting takes advantage of the static nature of microprocessor systems. It gives the troubleshooter enough time to trace the fault. You do not have to know software to apply SST effectively. Further, you do not have to learn new troubleshooting skills to have repeated success with the SST. You may simply apply old digital troubleshooting techniques to the microprocessor system troubleshooting problem.

CHAPTER 9

A MEMORY SYSTEM DIAGNOSTIC

9-1: INTRODUCTION

In this chapter, we will discuss a unique software routine. This software routine is designed to verify the operation of the system hardware—that is, hardware verification will be accomplished via software execution. The basic idea is to locate hardware fault sites by analyzing the way in which the system fails to execute software instructions. It should be pointed out that software diagnostics are of little value if the system under test is not capable of executing any code. This is perhaps the major shortcoming of troubleshooting techniques based on software diagnostics.

In the previous chapters of this text, we presented details on how to troubleshoot the main hardware of the 68000 system using Static Stimulus Testing. Note that Static Stimulus Testing is totally independent of software. In troubleshooting, a defective system must first be made to read data from system ROM. This is the troubleshooter's first step, the beginning point in the troubleshooting process. This can be accomplished using the SST. Once the system can read data from ROM, then the troubleshooter can write software to check other parts of the microprocessor system.

When troubleshooting microprocessor systems, one's objective is to get the system quickly to a point where the microprocessor can aid in the troubleshooting process. The Static Stimulus Tester is the easiest tool to accomplish this task. We will assume in this chapter that the hardware has been checked out and that the microprocessor system is capable of reading data back from system ROM. We will further assume that the microprocessor itself is not defective.

Let us now discuss a memory diagnostic. This test is designed to check all storage cells of a static or dynamic RAM system. If the system passes the test, the troubleshooter can have confidence that the RAM section of the system is operating correctly. If the test fails, the system will inform the troubleshooter of the defective address. Knowing the defective address will enable the troubleshooter to focus on the actual hardware chips that reside at this system address.

To begin, let us go over a flowchart of this memory test. After

BIT							
0	1	2	3	4	5	6	7

ADDRESS 0 →	1	1	1	1	1	1	1	1
ADDRESS 1	1	1	1	1	1	1	1	1
2	1	1	1	1	1	1	1	1
3	1	1	1	1	1	1	1	1
4	1	1	1	1	1	1	1	1
5	1	1	1	1	1	1	1	1
6	1	1	1	1	1	1	1	1
7	1	1	1	1	1	1	1	1
8	1	1	1	1	1	1	1	1
9	1	1	1	1	1	1	1	1

FIGURE 9–1.   The entire physical memory has logical 1's written into every memory location. This sample memory is organized as 10 address locations deep by 8-bits wide. The information in each address location is equal.

discussing the flowchart, we will realize each step with 68000 mnemonics. The memory test that we will use is called a "march test." This type of memory test is capable of uniquely determining if reading or writing to any memory location will disturb the information residing at other locations. To explain exactly what this means, consider the following.

Let us say we designed a memory test that will first write all 1's into the memory. The test will then read back the data and check to see if all 1's are in the memory. At the end of this test, we would like to have confidence that the memory system is good if the test passes. However, a test that does only what we just described will not do the job because, if all locations of the memory had logical 1's written into them, we could not distinguish one memory address from another. (See Fig. 9-1.) This means that the internal address decoders on the chip could be defective and the memory device would still read back logical 1's at each address. However, the logical 1's could keep coming from the same physical address inside the memory chip—that is, no address lines would need to be switching in the memory, yet the test will still pass. (See Fig. 9-2.)

Such a limited test has none of the unique qualities of a march pattern. Writing all 1's into a memory and then reading the 1's is

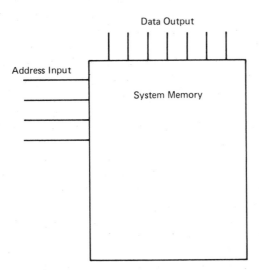

FIGURE 9–2. All physical address lines may be shorted to ground or stuck at logical 1. Even so, the memory device would still be outputting the expected data. Or, the data may all be coming from the same physical address instead of the one expected.

not a rigorous test for a microprocessor memory system to pass. A march pattern will remedy this weakness.

9-2: IMPLEMENTING A MARCH PATTERN

To explain exactly how the march pattern will work, let us show a small example. From this example, the testing scheme may be expanded to accommodate any length or width of memory system. We will assume that a 4 × 4 memory array is being used, as shown in Fig. 9-3.

First, a background of data of all 0's will be written into the memory.

The software will instruct the microprocessor to write all 0's into the memory space. After this operation, the 4 × 4 array will physically appear, as shown in Fig. 9-4.

Next, the microprocessor will read the background data from the first physical location. Data read from this location will be tested by the microprocessor to determine if it is a logical 0. If the data is a logical 0, then the memory READ operation was successful. The microprocessor will then write the complement data into the location just read. At the completion of this event, the physical memory will appear, as shown in Fig. 9-5.

The microprocessor will now perform the same operation on each successive memory cell—that is, the microprocessor will read the background data, test it for proper logic level, and then rewrite

```
X    X    X    X

X    X    X    X

X    X    X    X

X    X    X    X
```

FIGURE 9–3. A 4 × 4 memory array. Each "X" represents a physical memory cell in a semiconductor memory.

```
0    0    0    0

0    0    0    0

0    0    0    0

0    0    0    0
```

FIGURE 9–4. The memory array will have logical 0's written into each physical memory cell.

```
1    0    0    0

0    0    0    0

0    0    0    0

0    0    0    0
```

FIGURE 9–5. After each memory cell is tested, the complement data is written into the tested space. This shows how the memory will appear after the first cell is tested.

the opposite logical level to the memory location. This process will continue until all of the memory cells have been read and tested. Figure 9-6a,b shows how the data is written into memory. From this figure, you can see how the pattern is "marched" through the memory space.

After all of the memory has been read and written, the microprocessor will set up to execute another pass through the memory. Before we explain what the next pass of memory will be, let us discuss exactly what we have tested thus far.

At this point, we will assume that the memory has verified at each in the foregoing sequence. We have physically tested that each address location in the memory is capable of three hardware operations, which are:

1. The memory cell can store a logical 0.
2. A logical 0 can be read from the memory cell.
3. A logical 0 can be read from the memory cell and a logical 1 can be written to the memory cell without disturbing the data at any forward memory location. The term "forward location" refers to any memory cell that resides at an address greater than the cell under test.

```
1    1    1    0        1    1    1    1

0    0    0    0        1    1    1    1

0    0    0    0        1    1    1    1

0    0    0    0        1    1    0    0
```

          (a)   (b)

FIGURE 9–6a. This is how the 4 × 4 memory array will appear after three memory cells have been tested for a logical 0 and then have a logical 1 written into the cell.

FIGURE 9–6b. This figure shows how the memory array will appear after 14 memory cells have been tested. Notice how the logical 1's "march" through the memory.

```
0     0     0     0

0     1     1     1

1     1     1     1

1     1     1     1
```

FIGURE 9–7. This figure shows how the memory array will appear on the "second pass." The memory array has had 5 physical cells tested for logical 1 and replaced with a logical 0.

We have not yet checked the memory for backward disturbance. That is, the memory locations that are physically located at addresses behind the location under test may have been disturbed and data changed, but these are not checked on the first pass. We must ensure that no backward disturbance has occurred in the memory.

To accomplish this, another pass through the entire memory will be done. This time, the logical 1 is read at the memory location, and it is replaced with a logical 0. When the logical 1 is read from the memory cell and tests correctly, we have ensured that no backward disturbance has occurred. Figure 9-7 shows the pattern of testing on this second pass of the memory.

If the entire memory tests properly, the data stored at the end of the test will be the same as the background data that we had initially written into the memory.

Up to this point, we have indicated what we are testing in the memory. However, what if the data read back from the memory is not what we expected? What do we do if the test fails? If the test fails, we must have a way of determining at which address the failure occurred. Near the end of the software discussion, we will discuss exactly how you can accomplish this.

9-3:   THE MARCH PATTERN FLOWCHART

The flowchart for a march pattern is shown in Fig. 9-8. Let us discuss each step of this flowchart in detail so you may become sufficiently familiar with the logic of the flow to understand how the program may be implemented on another 68000 system.

Step A

The first step in the flowchart is the initialization section. In this section, the starting address of the memory test and the ending

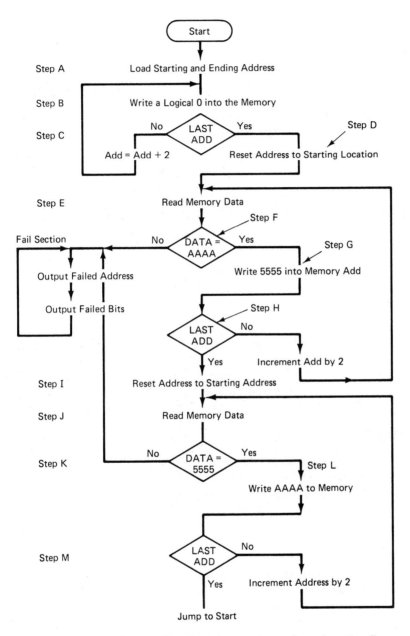

FIGURE 9–8. General flowchart for running a "march pattern" memory test.

address of the memory test will be placed into internal micro-processor registers. This is necessary because the system RAM space can be located anywhere in the microprocessor system. For our system, the RAM starting address will be 003000 and the RAM ending address will be 0037FF. This is the memory space that exists in the small system we have been discussing. The 68000 will read two bytes of memory during each memory READ operation. There-fore, the ending address we must use is 0037FE.

Step B

At this step in the flowchart, the microprocessor will write the background data into the memory address. The background data for this test will be AAAA. This word was chosen because it is an alternating pattern of 1 and 0 for data stored at a particular location.

Step C

This is the *decision block*. The microprocessor will test to see if this is the last address in the memory test space. If the test is false, then the system memory address is incremented by two and the microprocessor goes back to step B. If the test is true, we are at the last address, and the microprocessor will go to step D.

Step D

At this step, the microprocessor will reset the test address to the starting address of the memory space. By now, the micro-processor has written the background data AAAA into all memory locations between the lower and upper limits of the test space.

Step E

Now the microprocessor will read back the data at the memory location specified. This data will be the background data AAAA.

Step F

This is a decision block. The microprocessor will determine if the data read back from the memory location was as expected—that is, was the data read back equal to AAAA? If the data was not equal to AAAA, then the microprocessor will jump to the fail section of the program. (We will explain about the fail section at the end of this flowchart discussion.)

If the data read back from the memory was as expected, AAAA, the microprocessor will go to step G.

Step G

The data read back from the address under test was correct. The microprocessor will complement the data and write this new data into the address under test. The data that will now be in the memory location is 5555. This is the 1's complement of AAAA.

Step H

The microprocessor will not execute the decision block. The decision to be made is whether the address under test is the last one of the designated memory space to be tested. If the address is not the last one to be tested, the microprocessor will increment the address counter by two. The microprocessor will then jump back to step E. At this step, the microprocessor will again read data from memory.

If the microprocessor is at the last memory address to be tested, we know that the first pass through the memory was successful. We must now set up the microprocessor to prepare for the second pass.

Step I

The microprocessor will now reset the test address to the first address in the RAM test space. For our system, the address will be 003000.

Step J

The microprocessor will now read the data back from the memory. Recall that this is identical to step E. However, at this point, the microprocessor is expecting the data to be equal to 5555.

Step K

In this decision block, the microprocessor must determine if the data read back from the memory space was equal to 5555. If the data is not correct, the microprocessor will jump to the fail section of this program.

If the data read back from the memory is correct, the microprocessor will advance to step L.

Step L

In this step, the microprocessor will complement the data read back from the memory, and it will write this complemented data to memory. The data written to memory at this step will be AAAA. This is the 1's complement of the data 5555.

Step M

In this decision block, the microprocessor must determine if the test address has reached the upper limit. If this is true, then the memory has passed the entire test. In this case, the program can jump back to the start of the program. This will allow the system to execute the RAM test continually for an indefinite period of time. The program may also jump to any other program the system troubleshooter wishes.

If the address is not the last one to test, the microprocessor will increment the address count by 2, and then jump back to step J.

9-4:   FAIL SECTION OF THE FLOWCHART

If the system fails to read back the correct data, the microprocessor will jump to this section of the program. This section will do three things:

1. It will inform the troubleshooter that the test has failed.
2. It will indicate what address failed.
3. Further, it will indicate which data bits failed.

We will show how you can determine all three of these items of information by using only an oscilloscope. If the system has a CRT interface that is working, then the program can be made to write this information to the screen. We will assume that the system we are troubleshooting does not have a CRT interface that is working, or that the system does not require a CRT interface to function.

First, we wish to know if the test passed or failed. This can be done in the following way. We make the RAM test loop back to the start when it passed. This will allow the test to loop indefinitely, or until we force the system to execute another test.

With the system looping on the RAM test, the only control signals that will be active are the memory control signals—that is, we are not performing any I/O operations during this test. If the test is passing, then you can simply monitor the I/O request line, A23. If this line is always a logical 0, then the memory test has passed.

Using this simple control signal for a pass/fail indicator will work for other microprocessor-based systems also. We will assume that if the I/O request line is not active, the test has passed. The opposite of this statement is also true. If the I/O request line, A23, is ever a logical 1, then the test has failed. We have not yet shown how this is to be implemented with software.

If the memory test fails, then we want to know the defective address. Here is how that can be done: The address under test is contained in an internal register on the 68000. If the data read back from the memory was in error, we will jump to the fail section of code. All internal registers will retain the data that was contained in them at the time of the memory failure.

In the fail section of code, we can write the register that contains the memory address to an output port. The choice of the output port code is arbitrary. An output port that is not being used by the system for other hardware operations should be chosen. For example, let us choose output port address F00002.

We can "sync" our oscilloscope display on the A23 address line. When this line is a logical 1, the data on the data lines is equal to the address of the memory that failed the test. (See Fig. 9-9.)

A means has now been shown for indicating that the test has

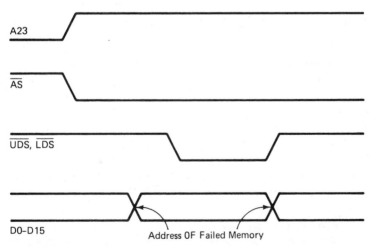

FIGURE 9–9. Timing diagram showing logical levels on the data output lines during an output *WRITE* operation. These lines will contain the logical address of the failed memory address during this output operation.

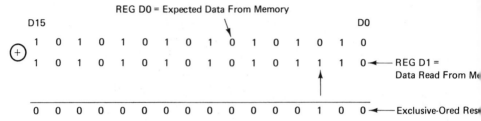

FIGURE 9–10. The expect data is stored in register D0. Data read back from memory is in register D1. When these two registers are exclusive-ored together the bits that do not match will be a logical 1. In this example, bit D02 did not match.

failed, and also for indicating which address was in error. The last piece of information we wish to obtain is what data bits failed. This can be accomplished in the following way.

At the time of the memory failure, the data read back from the system RAM was compared against the expected data. This means that both words were contained in some internal 68000 register. In the fail routine, we can exclusive-OR these two registers together. The result will be a logical 1 in each bit position where there was a failure. (See Fig. 9-10.)

The result of the exclusive-OR comparison will be stored in a 68000 register. We can output this data to an output port address.

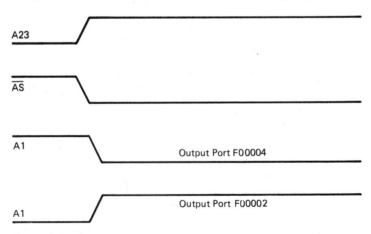

FIGURE 9–11. Address line A1 is a logical 0, when output port F00004 is writing data. This address line is used to indicate which type of data is on the system data bus. That is, when A1 is a logical 1 the data bus is outputting failed memory data bits. When A1 is a logical 0, the data bus is outputting the failed memory address.

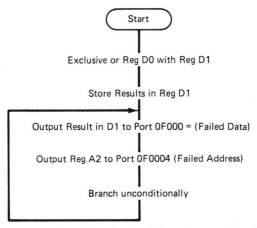

FIGURE 9–12. Flowchart for the fail routine section of code.

We will choose a different output port address than the one chosen for the outputting of the failed memory address, port F00002. We will use output port address F00004.

We choose the port address F00004 for a particular reason. If we examine the ports chosen, they differ in two bit positions—that is, A1 is a logical 1 for one address and A2 is a logical 1 for the other address. To determine which output port data is on the data bus at the time of an output WRITE operation, we can examine the logical state of address line A1 or A2. (See Fig. 9-11.)

During the time that A23 is a logical 1 and the address line A1 is a logical 1, the data on the system data bus will be the failed memory address. When A23 is a logical 1 and A2 is a logical 1, the data on the system data bus will be the failed data bits from RAM. The flowchart for realizing this fail routine is shown in Fig. 9-12.

The fail routine will be continually loop outputting the failed memory address and the failed data bits. The flowchart of the memory test is designed to stop on the first failure detected.

9-5: MNEMONICS FOR REALIZING THE FLOWCHART

A listing of the 68000 mnemonics that will realize the flowchart discussed in the previous section follows. Each step of the program is related to a step of the flowchart discussed previously.

```
 2
 3
 4*
 5*
 6*
 7
 8
 9
10
11
12*
13*
14*    START OF MAIN PROGRAM
15*
16*    THIS TEST WILL PERFORM A MARCH MEMORY TEST ON EACH
17*    WORD OF SYSTEM RAM. THE STARTING ADDRESS IS 4000.
18*    THE ENDING ADDRESS IS 7FFF. THE BACKGROUND DATA WILL
19*    BE AAAA AND 5555.
20*
21*    A0 = LOWER ADDRESS LIMIT
22*    A1 = UPPER ADDRESS LIMIT
23*    A2 = PRESENT ADDRESS OF TEST
24*    D0 = DATA FOR WRITE AND COMPARE
25*    D1 = DATA BACK FROM THE MEMORY TO TEST
26*
27*
28*    IF THE PROGRAM FAILS, IT WILL JUMP TO THE FAIL
29*    SECTION OF CODE. IF THE PROGRAM PASSES, IT WILL
30*    JUMP BACK TO THE START AND CONTINUALLY LOOP ON
31*    THE TEST.
```

```
32*
33*
34   0000  207C  0000  4000   MTEST   MOVE.L  #4000H,A0       SET LOWER LIMIT
35   0006  227C  0000  7FFF           MOVE.L  #7FFFH,A1       SET UPPER LIMIT
36   000C  203C  0000  AAAA           MOVE.L  #0AAAA,D0       SET BACK DATA
37   0012  3448                       MOVE    A0,A2           SET TEST ADD
38*  END OF THE INITIALIZATION. START OF THE WRITE LOOP
39*
40*
41   0014  3480           MWRIT       MOVE    D0,(A2)         DO TO A2 IND
42   0016  B4C9                       CMPA    A1,A2           LAST ADDRESS ??
43   0018  6704                       BEQ     LTEST           IF.EQ.THEN DONE
44   001A  544A                       ADDI    #2H,A2          INC TO NEXT WOR
45   001C  60FB                       BRA     MWRIT           DO THE NEXT WOR
46*
47*  FINISHED WRITING THE BACKGROUND DATA AAAA.
48*
49*  NOW TO START THE TESTING OF THE MEMORY
50*
51   001E  3448           LTEST       MOVE    A0,A2           RSET TEST ADD
52   0020  3212           LAGA        MOVE    (A2),D1         DATA TO A2 IND
53   0022  B041                       CMP     D1,D0           IS DATA GOOD ??
54   0024  6628                       BNE     MTAIL           IF.NE.THEN FAIL
55   0026  0A41  FFFF                 EORI    #0FFFFH,D1      INVERT THE DATA
56   002A  3481                       MOVE    D1,(A2)         WRITE INV DATA
57*
58*  A SINGLE ADDRESS HAS NOW BEEN TESTED, THE COMPLIMENT
59*  DATA HAS BEEN STORED IN THE LOCATION.
60*
61   002C  B2CA                       CMPA    A2,A1           LAST ADDRESS ??
62   002E  6704                       BEQ     BACKD           IF.EQ.DONE
```

175

```
63   0030  544A        ADDI   #2H,A2        A2=NEXT WORD
64   0032  60EC        BRA    LAGA          DO THE NEXT WOR
65*
66*  AT THIS POINT IN THE PROGRAM WE HAVE FINISHED
67*  A SINGLE PASS ON THE MEMORY. THE DATA IN
68*  MEMORY IS NOW EQUAL TO 5555 AT EVERY LOCATION.
69*  WE MAKE ANOTHER PASS TESTING FOR THIS DATA.
70*
71*
72   0034  3448    BACKD  MOVE  A0,A2          RESET TEST ADD
73   0036  0A40 FFFF      EORI  #0FFFFH,D0     INV TEST DATA
74   003A  3212    BACK1  MOVE  (A2),D1        GET MEMORY DATA
75   003C  B041           CMP   D1,D0          DATA GOOD ????
76   003E  660E           BNE   MTAIL          IF.NE.THEN FAIL
77*
78*
79*  AT THIS POINT WE HAVE TESTED A SINGLE MEMORY LOCATION
80*  WE MUST INVERT THE MEMORY DATA AND WRITE IT BACK TO
81*  THE MEMORY ADDRESS WE HAVE JUST TESTED.
82*
83*
84   0040  0A41 FFFF      EOR1  #0FFFFH,D1     INV MEMORY DATA
85   0044  3481           MOVE  D1,(A2)        WRITE DAT TO MB
86   0046  B2CA           CMP   A2,A1          LAST ADDRESS ??
87   0048  67B6           BEQ   MTEST          IF.EQ. PASS
88   004A  549A           ADDI  #2H,A2         A2 = NEXT ADD
89   004C  60EC           BRA   BACK1          DO NEXT ADD
90*
```

```
 91*
 92*          AT THIS POINT WE HAVE TESTED THE ENTIRE MEMORY.
 93*          IF THE TEST PASSES, THE PROGRAM WILL LOOP BACK TO
 94*          MTEST. THIS WILL START THE EXECUTION OF THE PROGRAM
 95*          OVER FROM THE START.
 96*
 97*          IF THE TEST FAILS, THEN THE PROGRAM WILL WRITE THE FAILED
 98*          BITS AND ADDRESS USING THE MTAIL SECTION OF CODE.
 99*
100*
101*          THIS IS THE MTAIL SECTION OF THE PROGRAM. IN THIS
102*          SECTION WE WILL HANDLE THE FAIL OF A MEMORY ADDRESS.
103*          THE PROGRAM WILL WRITE THE FAILED ADDRESS TO PORT
104*          0F0004. THE FAILED DATA BITS WILL BE WRITTEN TO PORT
105*          0F0002.
106*
107*
108*
109   004E  B141                  MTAIL   EOR    D0,D1         GET THE FAILED BITS INTO
110   0050  207C  000F  0002       MF1    MOVE.L #0F0002H,A0
111   0056  3081                          MOVE   D1,(A0)       OUTPUT FAILED DATA
112   0058  5448                          ADDI   #2H,A0
113   005A  308A                          MOVE   A2,(A0)       OUTPUT FAILED ADDRESS
114   005C  60F2                          BRA    MF1           LOOP ON MTAIL
115*
116   005E  0000                          END

0 ERRORS
```

9-6: CHAPTER SUMMARY

A basic question facing the microprocessor system trouble-shooter is whether a malfunction is due to software or hardware. If the system once worked, it is unlikely to be a software problem. If the system has not yet worked, as in a newly built or prototype system, the basic question must be faced. If it can be proven that either the software or hardware works, the process is cut in half. With Static Stimulus Testing, verification of hardware operation can be made independently of software. (The single exception is the hardware verification of a dynamic RAM cell.)

In this chapter, we assumed that a section of the system hardware was operational. This section allows the microprocessor to read data from ROM. We can verify this using SST techniques. With this part of the system operational, we cannot let the microprocessor aid us in further troubleshooting via software diagnostics.

The reason we turn to software diagnostics at this point is that it will save us time. A major reason for checking ROM with SST techniques originally is that we could not apply software diagnostics if the microprocessor cannot read data from ROM.

A march pattern software diagnostic is equally effective for both static and dynamic memory systems. While the software presented here applies only to the 68000, the concept can be used with any 8- or 16-bit microprocessor system.

APPENDIX

PIN ASSIGNMENTS (TOP VIEWS)

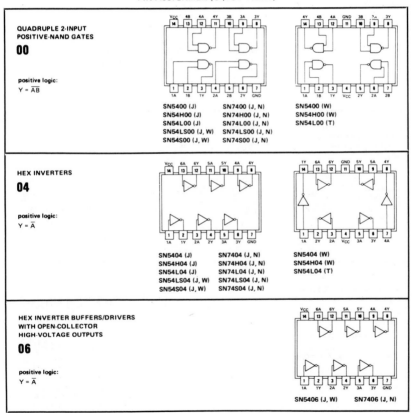

QUADRUPLE 2-INPUT POSITIVE-NAND GATES

00

positive logic:
$Y = \overline{AB}$

SN5400 (J)	SN7400 (J, N)
SN54H00 (J)	SN74H00 (J, N)
SN54L00 (J)	SN74L00 (J, N)
SN54LS00 (J, W)	SN74LS00 (J, N)
SN54S00 (J, W)	SN74S00 (J, N)

SN5400 (W)
SN54H00 (W)
SN54L00 (T)

HEX INVERTERS

04

positive logic:
$Y = \overline{A}$

SN5404 (J)	SN7404 (J, N)
SN54H04 (J)	SN74H04 (J, N)
SN54L04 (J)	SN74L04 (J, N)
SN54LS04 (J, W)	SN74LS04 (J, N)
SN54S04 (J, W)	SN74S04 (J, N)

SN5404 (W)
SN54H04 (W)
SN54L04 (T)

HEX INVERTER BUFFERS/DRIVERS WITH OPEN-COLLECTOR HIGH-VOLTAGE OUTPUTS

06

positive logic:
$Y = \overline{A}$

SN5406 (J, W)   SN7406 (J, N)

The figures on pages 179–182 are from "The TTL Data Book for Design Engineers." © 1981, Texas Instruments Incorporated.

PIN ASSIGNMENTS (TOP VIEWS)

QUADRUPLE 2-INPUT POSITIVE-AND GATES

08

positive logic:
Y = AB

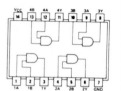

SN5408 (J, W)   SN7408 (J, N)
SN54LS08 (J, W)   SN74LS08 (J, N)
SN54S08 (J, W)   SN74S08 (J, N)

8-INPUT POSITIVE-NAND GATES

30

positive logic:
Y = $\overline{ABCDEFGH}$

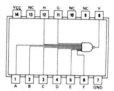

SN5430 (J)   SN7430 (J, N)   SN5430 (W)
SN54H30 (J)   SN74H30 (J, N)   SN54H30 (W)
SN54L30 (J)   SN74L30 (J, N)   SN54L30 (T)
SN54LS30 (J, W)   SN74LS30 (J, N)
SN54S30 (J, W)   SN74S30 (J, N)   NC—No internal connection

QUADRUPLE 2-INPUT POSITIVE-OR GATES

32

positive logic:
Y = A+B

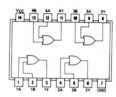

SN5432 (J, W)   SN7432 (J, N)
SN54LS32 (J, W)   SN74LS32 (J, N)
SN54S32 (J, W)   SN74S32 (J, N)

---

4 LINE-TO-10-LINE DECODERS

42 BCD-TO-DECIMAL

43 EXCESS-3-TO-DECIMAL

44 EXCESS-3-GRAY-TO-DECIMAL

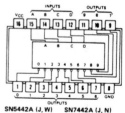

SN5442A (J, W)   SN7442A (J, N)
SN54L42 (J)   SN74L42 (J, N)
SN54LS42 (J, W)   SN74LS42 (J, N)
SN5443A (J, W)   SN7443A (J, N)
SN54L43 (J)   SN74L43 (J, N)
SN5444A (J, W)   SN7444A (J, N)
SN54L44 (J)   SN74L44 (J, N)

PIN ASSIGNMENTS (TOP VIEW)

3- TO 8-LINE DECODERS/DEMULTIPLEXERS

138

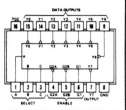

SN54LS138 (J, W)   SN74LS138 (J, N)
SN54S138 (J, W)   SN74S138 (J, N)

PRESETABLE COUNTERS/LATCHES

196   DECADE/BI-QUINARY

197   BINARY

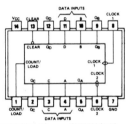

SN54196 (J, W)   SN74196 (J, N)
SN54LS196 (J, W)   SN74LS196 (J, N)
SN54S196 (J, W)   SN74S196 (J, N)
SN54197 (J, W)   SN74197 (J, N)
SN54LS197 (J, W)   SN74LS197 (J, N)
SN54S197 (J, W)   SN74S197 (J, N)

OCTAL BUFFERS/LINE DRIVERS/LINE RECEIVERS

240   INVERTED 3-STATE OUTPUTS

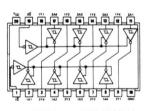

SN54LS240 (J)   SN74LS240 (J, N)
SN54S240 (J)   SN74S240 (J, N)

OCTAL BUFFERS/LINE DRIVERS/LINE RECEIVERS

244   NONINVERTED 3-STATE OUTPUTS

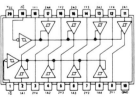

SN54LS244 (J)   SN74LS244 (J, N)

PIN ASSIGNMENTS (TOP VIEWS)

OCTAL BUS TRANCEIVERS

245 NONINVERTED 3-STATE OUTPUTS

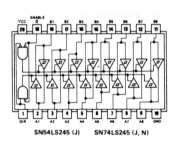

SN54LS245 (J)   SN74LS245 (J, N)

QUAD $\overline{S}$-$\overline{R}$ LATCHES

279 DIODE-CLAMPED INPUTS
TOTEM-POLE OUTPUTS

H = high level
L = low level

FUNCTION TABLE		
INPUTS		OUTPUT
$\overline{S}$†	$\overline{R}$	Q
H	H	Q_0
L	H	H
H	L	L
L	L	H*

Q_0 = the level of Q before the indicated input conditions were established.
* This output level is pseudo stable; that is, it may not persist when the $\overline{S}$ and $\overline{R}$ inputs return to their inactive (high) level.
† For latches with double $\overline{S}$ inputs:
 H = both $\overline{S}$ inputs high
 L = one or both $\overline{S}$ inputs low

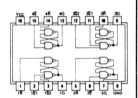

SN54279 (J, W)   SN74279 (J, N)
SN54LS279 (J, W) SN74LS279 (J, N)

OCTAL D-TYPE LATCHES

373 3-STATE OUTPUTS
COMMON OUTPUT CONTROL
COMMON ENABLE

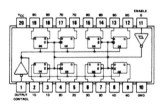

SN54LS373 (J)   SN74LS373 (J, N)
SN54S373 (J)   SN74S373 (J, N)

OCTAL D-TYPE FLIP-FLOPS

374 3-STATE OUTPUTS
COMMON OUTPUT CONTROL
COMMON CLOCK

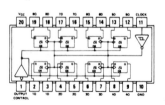

SN54LS374 (J)   SN74LS374 (J, N)
SN54S374 (J)   SN74S374 (J, N)

 **MOTOROLA**

MCM2716
MCM27L16

2048 × 8-BIT UV ERASABLE PROM

The MCM2716/27L16 is a 16,384-bit Erasable and Electrically Reprogrammable PROM designed for system debug usage and similar applications requiring nonvolatile memory that could be reprogrammed periodically. The transparent lid on the package allows the memory content to be erased with ultraviolet light.

For ease of use, the device operates from a single power supply and has a static power-down mode. Pin-for-pin mask programmable ROMs are available for large volume production runs of systems initially using the MCM2716/27L16.

- Single 5 V Power Supply
- Automatic Power-down Mode (Standby)
- Organized as 2048 Bytes of 8 Bits
- Low Power Version 27L16/27L16-35 Active 50 mA Max
  Standby 10 mA Max
  27L16-25 Active 70 mA Max
  Standby 15 mA Max
- TTL Compatible During Read and Program
- Maximum Access Time = 450 ns MCM2716
  350 ns MCM2716-35
  250 ns MCM2716-25
- Pin Equivalent to Intel's 2716
- Pin Compatible to MCM68A316E
- Output Enable Active Level is User Selectable

MOS
(N-CHANNEL, SILICON-GATE)

2048 × 8-BIT
UV ERASABLE PROM

C SUFFIX
FRIT-SEAL CERAMIC PACKAGE
CASE 623A

L SUFFIX CERAMIC PACKAGE
ALSO AVAILABLE — CASE 716

PIN ASSIGNMENT

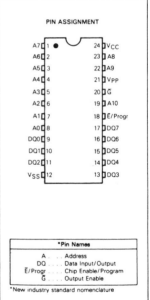

A7	1	24	Vcc
A6	2	23	A8
A5	3	22	A9
A4	4	21	Vpp
A3	5	20	Ḡ
A2	6	19	A10
A1	7	18	Ē/Progr
A0	8	17	DQ7
DQ0	9	16	DQ6
DQ1	10	15	DQ5
DQ2	11	14	DQ4
VSS	12	13	DQ3

*Pin Names	
A	Address
DQ	Data Input/Output
Ē/Progr	Chip Enable/Program
Ḡ	Output Enable

*New industry standard nomenclature

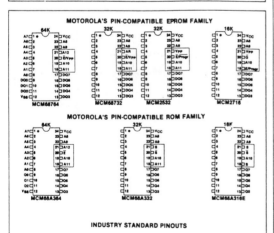

MOTOROLA'S PIN-COMPATIBLE EPROM FAMILY

64K — MCM68764 32K — MCM68732 32K — MCM2532 16K — MCM2716

MOTOROLA'S PIN-COMPATIBLE ROM FAMILY

64K — MCM68A364 32K — MCM68A332 16K — MCM68A316E

INDUSTRY STANDARD PINOUTS

ABSOLUTE MAXIMUM RATINGS

Rating	Value	Unit
Temperature Under Bias	− 10 to + 80	°C
Operating Temperature Range	0 to + 70	°C
Storage Temperature	− 65 to + 125	°C
All Input or Output Voltages with Respect to V_{SS}	+ 6 to − 0.3	Vdc
Vpp Supply Voltage with Respect to $\overline{G}$	+ 28 to − 0.3	Vdc

NOTE: Permanent device damage may occur if ABSOLUTE MAXIMUM RATINGS are exceeded. Functional operation should be restricted to RECOMMENDED OPERATING CONDITIONS. Exposure to higher than recommended voltages for extended periods of time could affect device reliability.

This device contains circuitry to protect the inputs against damage due to high static voltages or electric fields; however, it is advised that normal precautions be taken to avoid application of any voltage higher than maximum rated voltages to this high-impedance circuit.

MODE SELECTION

Mode	9-11, 13-17 DQ	12 V_{SS}	18 E/Progr	20 G*	21 Vpp	24 Vcc
				Pin Number		
Read	Data Out	V_{SS}	V_{IL}	V_{IL}	V_{CC}^*	V_{CC}
Output Disable	High Z	V_{SS}	Don't Care	V_{IH}	V_{CC}^*	V_{CC}
Standby	High Z	V_{SS}	V_{IH}	Don't Care	V_{CC}^*	V_{CC}
Program	Data In	V_{SS}	Pulsed V_{IL} to V_{IH}	V_{IH}	V_{IHP}	V_{CC}
Program Verify	Data Out	V_{SS}	V_{IL}	V_{IL}	V_{IHP}	V_{CC}
Program Inhibit	High Z	V_{SS}	V_{IL}	V_{IH}	V_{IHP}	V_{CC}

*In the Read Mode if $V_{PP} \geq V_{IH}$, then $\overline{G}$ (active low)
  $V_{PP} \leq V_{IL}$, then G (active high)

BLOCK DIAGRAM

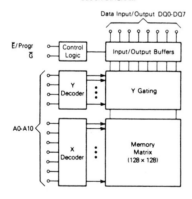

Data Input/Output DQ0-DQ7

E/Progr
$\overline{G}$

A0-A10

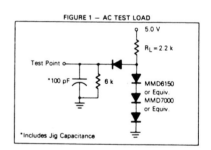

FIGURE 1 — AC TEST LOAD

5.0 V

$R_L = 2.2$ k

Test Point

*100 pF   6 k

MMD6150 or Equiv.
MMD7000 or Equiv.

*Includes Jig Capacitance

MCM2716•MCM27L16

CAPACITANCE (f = 1.0 MHz, T_A = 25°C, periodically sampled rather than 100% tested)

Characteristic	Symbol	Typ	Max	Unit
Input Capacitance (V_{in} = 0 V)	C_{in}	4.0	6.0	pF
Output Capacitance (V_{out} = 0 V)	C_{out}	8.0	12	pF

Capacitance measured with a Boonton Meter or effective capacitance calculated from the equation: $C = \dfrac{I \Delta t}{\Delta V}$

DC OPERATING CONDITIONS AND CHARACTERISTICS
(Full operating voltage and temperature range unless otherwise noted)

RECOMMENDED DC READ OPERATING CONDITIONS

Parameter		Symbol	Min	Nom	Max	Unit
Supply Voltage*	MCM2716	V_{CC}	4.75	5.0	5.25	V
		V_{PP}	4.75	5.0	5.25	
Input High Voltage		V_{IH}	2.0	—	V_{CC} + 1.0	V
Input Low Voltage		V_{IL}	−0.1	—	0.8	V

RECOMMENDED DC OPERATING CHARACTERISTICS

Characteristic		Condition	Symbol	MCM2716			Units
				Min	Typ	Max	
Address, $\overline{G}$ and $\overline{E}$/Progr Input Sink Current		V_{in} = 5.25 V	I_{in}	—	—	10	μA
Output Leakage Current		V_{out} = 5.25 V $\overline{G}$ = 5.0 V	I_{LO}	—	—	10	μA
V_{CC} Supply Current (Standby) 2716		$\overline{E}$/Progr = V_{IH} $\overline{G}$ = V_{IL}	I_{CC1}	—	—	25	mA
V_{CC} Supply Current (Active) 2716	(Outputs Open)	$\overline{G}$ = $\overline{E}$/Progr = V_{IL}	I_{CC2}	—	—	100	mA
Vpp Supply Current*		V_{PP} = 5.25 V	I_{PP1}	—	—	5.0	mA
Output Low Voltage		I_{OL} = 2.1 mA	V_{OL}	—	—	0.45	V
Output High Voltage		I_{OH} = −400 μA	V_{OH}	2.4	—	—	V

*V_{CC} must be applied simultaneously or prior to Vpp. V_{CC} must also be switched off simultaneously with or after Vpp. With Vpp connected directly to V_{CC} during the read operation, the supply current would then be the sum of I_{PP1} and I_{CC}.

AC OPERATING CONDITIONS AND CHARACTERISTICS
(Full operating voltage and temperature range unless otherwise noted)

Input Pulse Levels . . . . 0.8 Volt and 2.2 Volts   Input and Output Timing Levels . . . . 2.0 and 0.8 Volts
Input Rise and Fall Times . . . . 20 ns   Output Load . . . . See Figure 1

Characteristic	Condition	Symbol	MCM2716		Units
			Min	Max	
Address Valid to Output Valid	$\overline{E}$/Progr = $\overline{G}$ = V_{IL}	t_{AVQV}	—	450	ns
$\overline{E}$/Progr to Output Valid	(Note 2)	t_{ELQV}	—	450	
Output Enable to Output Valid	$\overline{E}$/Progr = V_{IL}	t_{GLQV}	—	150	
$\overline{E}$/Progr to High Z Output	—	t_{EHQZ}	0	100	
Output Disable to High Z Output	$\overline{E}$/Progr = V_{IL}	t_{GHQZ}	0	100	
Data Hold from Address	$\overline{E}$/Progr = $\overline{G}$ = V_{IL}	t_{AXDX}	0	—	

MCM2716•MCM27L16

READ MODE TIMING DIAGRAMS ($\overline{E}$/Progr = V_{IL})

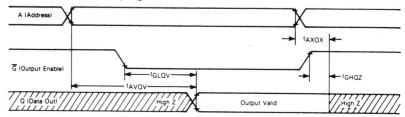

STANDBY MODE (Output Enable = V_{IL})
Standby Mode ($\overline{E}$/Progr = V_{IH})

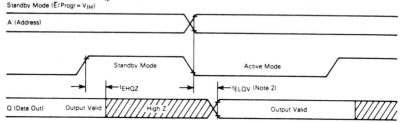

NOTE 2: t_{ELQV} is referenced to $\overline{E}$/Progr or stable address, whichever occurs last.

DC PROGRAMMING CONDITIONS AND CHARACTERISTICS
($T_A = 25°C \pm 5°C$)

RECOMMENDED PROGRAMMING OPERATING CONDITIONS

Parameter	Symbol	Min	Nom	Max	Unit
Supply Voltage	V_{CC}	4.75	5.0	5.25	Vdc
	V_{PP}	24	25	26	
Input High Voltage for Data	V_{IH}	2.2	–	V_{CC} + 1	Vdc
Input Low Voltage for Data	V_{IL}	– 0.1	–	0.8	Vdc

PROGRAMMING OPERATION DC CHARACTERISTICS

Characteristic	Condition	Symbol	Min	Typ	Max	Unit
Address, $\overline{G}$ and $\overline{E}$/Progr Input Sink Current	V_{in} = 5.25 V/0.45 V	I_{LI}	–	–	10	μAdc
V_{PP} Supply Current (V_{PP} = 25 V ± 1 V)	$\overline{E}$/Progr = V_{IL}	I_{PP1}	–	–	10	mAdc
V_{PP} Programming Pulse Supply Current (V_{PP} = 25 V ± 1 V)	$\overline{E}$/Progr = V_{IH}	I_{PP2}	–	–	30	mAdc
V_{CC} Supply Current (Outputs Open)	–	I_{CC}	–	–	160	mAdc

AC PROGRAMMING OPERATING CONDITIONS AND CHARACTERISTICS

Characteristic	Symbol	Min	Max	Unit
Address Setup Time	t_{AVEH}	2.0	–	μS
Output Enable High to Program Pulse	t_{GHEH}	2.0	–	μS
Data Setup Time	t_{DVEH}	2.0	–	μS
Address Hold Time	t_{ELAX}	2.0	–	μS
Output Enable Hold Time	t_{ELGL}	2.0	–	μS
Data Hold Time	t_{ELQZ}	2.0	–	μS
Vpp Setup Time	t_{PHEH}	0	–	ns
Vpp to Enable Low Time	t_{ELPL}	0	–	ns
Output Disable to High Z Output	t_{GHQZ}	0	150	ns
Output Enable to Valid Data ($\overline{E}$/Progr = V_{IL})	t_{GLQV}	–	150	ns
Program Pulse Width	t_{EHEL}	1*	55	ms
Program Pulse Rise Time	t_{PR}	5	–	ns
Program Pulse Fall Time	t_{PF}	5	–	ns

*If shorter than 45 ms (min) pulses are used, the same number of pulses should be applied after the specific data has been verified.

MCM2716•MCM27L16

PROGRAMMING OPERATION TIMING DIAGRAM

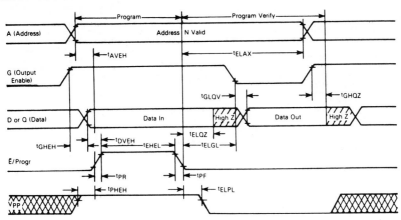

PROGRAMMING INSTRUCTIONS

After the completion of an ERASE operation, every bit in the device is in the "1" state (represented by Output High). Data are entered by programming zeros (Output Low) into the required bits. The words are addressed the same way as in the READ operation. A programmed "0" can only be changed to a "1" by ultraviolet light erasure.

To set the memory up for Program Mode, the Vpp input (Pin 21) should be raised to + 25 V. The V_{CC} supply voltage is the same as for the Read operation and G is at V_{IH}. Programming data is entered in 8-bit words through the data out (DQ) terminals. Only "0's" will be programmed when "0's" and "1's" are entered in the 8-bit data word.

After address and data setup, a program pulse (V_{IL} to V_{IH}) is applied to the Ē/Progr input. A program pulse is applied to each address location to be programmed. To minimize programming time, a 2 ms pulse width is recommended. The maximum program pulse width is 55 ms; therefore, programming must not be attempted with a dc signal applied to the Ē/Progr input.

Multiple MCM2716s may be programmed in parallel by connecting together like inputs and applying the program pulse to the Ē/Progr inputs. Different data may be programmed into multiple MCM2716s connected in parallel by using the PROGRAM INHIBIT mode. Except for the Ē/Progr pin, all like inputs (including Output Enable) may be common.

The PROGRAM VERIFY mode with Vpp at 25 V is used to determine that all programmed bits were correctly programmed.

READ OPERATION

After access time, data is valid at the outputs in the READ mode. With stable system addresses, effectively faster access time can be obtained by gating the data onto the bus with Output Enable.

The Standby mode is available to reduce active power dissipation. The outputs are in the high impedance state when the Ē/Progr input pin is high (V_{IH}) independent of the Output Enable input.

ERASING INSTRUCTIONS

The MCM2716/27L16 can be erased by exposure to high intensity shortwave ultraviolet light, with a wavelength of 2537 angstroms. The recommended integrated dose (i.e., UV-intensity X exposure time) is 15 Ws/cm². As an example, using the "Model 30-000" UV-Eraser (Turner Designs, Mountain View, CA 94043) the ERASE-time is 36 minutes. The lamps should be used without shortwave filters and the MCM2716/MCM27L16 should be positioned about one inch away from the UV-tubes.

MCM2716•MCM27L16

TIMING PARAMETER ABBREVIATIONS

t X X X X

signal name from which interval is defined
transition direction for first signal
signal name to which interval is defined
transition direction for second signal

The transition definitions used in this data sheet are:

H = transition to high
L = transition to low
V = transition to valid
X = transition to invalid or don't care
Z = transition to off (high impedance)

TIMING LIMITS

The table of timing values shows either a minimum or a maximum limit for each parameter. Input requirements are specified from the external system point of view. Thus, address setup time is shown as a minimum since the system must supply at least that much time (even though most devices do not require it). On the other hand, responses from the memory are specified from the device point of view. Thus, the access time is shown as a maximum since the device never provides data later than that time.

WAVEFORMS

Waveform Symbol	Input	Output
	Must Be Valid	Will Be Valid
	Change From H to L	Will Change From H to L
	Change From L to H	Will Change From L to H
	Don't Care Any Change Permitted	Changing State Unknown
		High Impedance

 **MOTOROLA**

MCM2114
MCM21L14

4096-BIT STATIC RANDOM ACCESS MEMORY

The MCM2114 is a 4096-bit random access memory fabricated with high density, high reliability N-channel silicon-gate technology. For ease of use, the device operates from a single power supply, is directly compatible with TTL and DTL, and requires no clocks or refreshing because of fully static operation. Data access is particularly simple, since address setup times are not required. The output data has the same polarity as the input data.

The MCM2114 is designed for memory applications where simple interfacing is the design objective. The MCM2114 is assembled in 18-pin dual-in-line packages with the industry standard pin-out. A separate chip select ($\overline{S}$) lead allows easy selection of an individual package when the three-state outputs are OR-tied.

The MCM2114 series has a maximum current of 100 mA. Low power versions (i.e., MCM21L14 series) are available with a maximum current of only 70 mA.

- 1024 Words by 4-Bit Organization
- Industry Standard 18-Pin Configuration
- Single +5 Volt Supply
- No Clock or Timing Strobe Required
- Fully Static: Cycle Time = Access Time
- Maximum Access Time
  MCM2114-20/MCM21L14-20 200 ns
  MCM2114-25/MCM21L14-25 250 ns
  MCM2114-30/MCM21L14-30 300 ns
  MCM2114-45/MCM21L14-45 450 ns
- Fully TTL Compatible
- Common Data Input and Output
- Three-State Outputs for OR-Ties
- Low Power Version Available

MOS
(N-CHANNEL, SILICON-GATE)

4096-BIT STATIC RANDOM ACCESS MEMORY

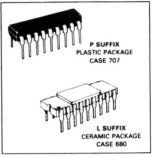

P SUFFIX
PLASTIC PACKAGE
CASE 707

L SUFFIX
CERAMIC PACKAGE
CASE 680

PIN ASSIGNMENT

A6	1	18	VCC
A5	2	17	A7
A4	3	16	A8
A3	4	15	A9
A0	5	14	DQ1
A1	6	13	DQ2
A2	7	12	DQ3
$\overline{S}$	8	11	DQ4
VSS	9	10	$\overline{W}$

PIN NAMES	
A0-A9	Address Input
$\overline{W}$	Write Enable
$\overline{S}$	Chip Select
DQ1-DQ4	Data Input/Output
VCC	Power (+5 V)
VSS	Ground

BLOCK DIAGRAM

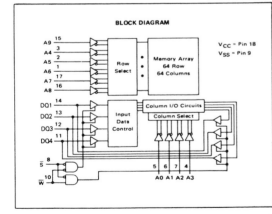

MCM2114•MCM21L14

ABSOLUTE MAXIMUM RATINGS (See Note)

Rating	Value	Unit
Temperature Under Bias	– 10 to + 80	°C
Voltage on Any Pin With Respect to V_{SS}	– 0.5 to + 7.0	V
DC Output Current	5.0	mA
Power Dissipation	1.0	Watt
Operating Temperature Range	0 to + 70	°C
Storage Temperature Range	– 65 to + 150	°C

NOTE: Permanent device damage may occur if ABSOLUTE MAXIMUM RATINGS are exceeded. Functional operation should be restricted to RECOMMENDED OPERATING CONDITIONS. Exposure to higher than recommended voltages for extended periods of time could affect device reliability

> This device contains circuitry to protect the inputs against damage due to high static voltages or electric fields, however, it is advised that normal precautions be taken to avoid application of any voltage higher than maximum rated voltages to this high-impedance circuit

DC OPERATING CONDITIONS AND CHARACTERISTICS
(Full operating voltage and temperature range unless otherwise noted.)

RECOMMENDED DC OPERATING CONDITIONS

Parameter	Symbol	Min	Typ	Max	Unit
Supply Voltage	V_{CC}	4.75	5.0	5.25	V
	V_{SS}	0	0	0	
Logic 1 Voltage, All Inputs	V_{IH}	2.0	–	6.0	V
Logic 0 Voltage, All Inputs	V_{IL}	– 0.5		0.8	V

DC CHARACTERISTICS

Parameter	Symbol	MCM2114 Min	MCM2114 Typ	MCM2114 Max	MCM21L14 Min	MCM21L14 Typ	MCM21L14 Max	Unit
Input Load Current (All Input Pins, $V_{in} = 0$ to 5.5 V)	I_{LI}	–	–	10	–	–	10	μA
I/O Leakage Current ($\overline{S} = 2.4$ V, $V_{DQ} = 0.4$ V to V_{CC})	I_{ILOi}	–	–	10	–	–	10	μA
Power Supply Current ($V_{in} = 5.5$ V, $I_{DQ} = 0$ mA, $T_A = 25°C$)	I_{CC1}	–	80	95	–	–	65	mA
Power Supply Current ($V_{in} = 5.5$ V, $I_{DQ} = 0$ mA, $T_A = 0°C$)	I_{CC2}	–	–	100	–	–	70	mA
Output Low Current $V_{OL} = 0.4$ V	I_{OL}	2.1	6.0	–	2.1	6.0	–	mA
Output High Current $V_{OH} = 2.4$ V	I_{OH}	–	– 1.4	– 1.0	–	– 1.4	– 1.0	mA

NOTE: Duration not to exceed 30 seconds.

CAPACITANCE (f = 1.0 MHz, $T_A = 25°C$, periodically sampled rather than 100% tested)

Characteristic	Symbol	Max	Unit
Input Capacitance ($V_{in} = 0$ V)	C_{in}	5.0	pF
Input/Output Capacitance ($V_{DQ} = 0$ V)	$C_{I/O}$	5.0	pF

Capacitance measured with a Boonton Meter or effective capacitance calculated from the equation: $C = I\Delta_t/\Delta V$

AC OPERATING CONDITIONS AND CHARACTERISTICS
(Full operating voltage and temperature unless otherwise noted.)

Input Pulse Levels	0.8 Volt to 2.4 Volts	Input and Output Timing Levels	1.5 Volts
Input Rise and Fall Times	10 ns	Output Load	1 TTL Gate and $C_L = 100$ pF

READ (NOTE 1), WRITE (NOTE 2) CYCLES

Parameter	Symbol	MCM2114-20 MCM21L14-20 Min	MCM2114-20 MCM21L14-20 Max	MCM2114-25 MCM21L14-25 Min	MCM2114-25 MCM21L14-25 Max	MCM2114-30 MCM21L14-30 Min	MCM2114-30 MCM21L14-30 Max	MCM2114-45 MCM21L14-45 Min	MCM2114-45 MCM21L14-45 Max	Unit
Address Valid to Address Don't Care	t_{AVAX}	200	–	250	–	300	–	450	–	ns
Address Valid to Output Valid	t_{AVQV}	–	200	–	250	–	300	–	450	ns
Chip Select Low to Data Valid	t_{SLQV}	–	70	–	85	–	100	–	120	ns
Chip Select Low to Output Don't Care	t_{SLQX}	20	–	20	–	20	–	20	–	ns
Chip Select High to Output High Z	t_{SHQZ}	–	60	–	70	–	80	–	100	ns
Address Don't Care to Output High Z	t_{AXQZ}	50	–	50	–	50	–	50	–	ns
Write Low to Write High	t_{WLWH}	120	–	135	–	150	–	200	–	ns
Write High to Address Don't Care	t_{WHAX}	0	–	0	–	0	–	0	–	ns
Write Low to Output High Z	t_{WLQZ}	–	60	–	70	–	80	–	100	ns
Data Valid to Write High	t_{DVWH}	120	–	135	–	150	–	200	–	ns
Write High to Data Don't	t_{WHDX}	0	–	0	–	0	–	0	–	ns

NOTES: 1. A Read occurs during the overlap of a low $\overline{S}$ and a high $\overline{W}$.
2. A Write occurs during the overlap of a low $\overline{S}$ and a low $\overline{W}$.

MCM2114•MCM21L14

READ CYCLE TIMING ($\overline{W}$ HELD HIGH)

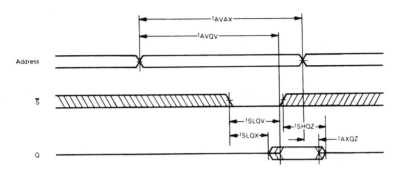

WRITE CYCLE TIMING (NOTE 3)

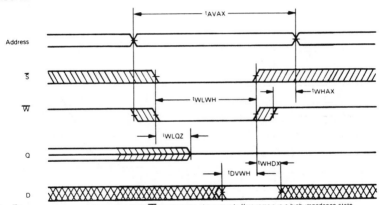

3 If the $\overline{S}$ low transition occurs simultaneously with the $\overline{W}$ low transition, the output buffers remain in a high-impedance state.

WAVEFORMS

Waveform Symbol	Input	Output
———	MUST BE VALID	WILL BE VALID
\\\\\\\	CHANGE FROM H TO L	WILL CHANGE FROM H TO L
/////	CHANGE FROM L TO H	WILL CHANGE FROM L TO H
XXXXX	DON'T CARE ANY CHANGE PERMITTED	CHANGING STATE UNKNOWN
⟩——⟨		HIGH IMPEDANCE

TYPICAL CHARACTERISTICS

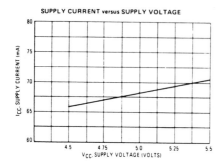

SUPPLY CURRENT versus SUPPLY VOLTAGE

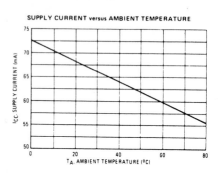

SUPPLY CURRENT versus AMBIENT TEMPERATURE

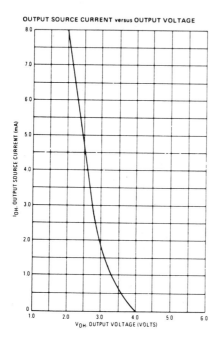

OUTPUT SOURCE CURRENT versus OUTPUT VOLTAGE

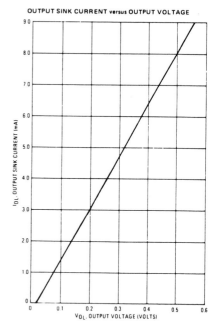

OUTPUT SINK CURRENT versus OUTPUT VOLTAGE

MCM2114•MCM21L14

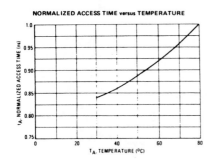

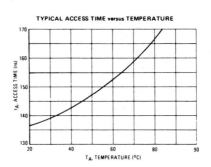

MCM2114/MCM21L14 BIT MAP

PIN 1

PIN 18
V_{CC}

1023◄────────1008	1023◄────────1008	1023◄────────1008	1023◄────────1008
1007	1007	1007	1007
DQ3 (PIN NO. 12)	DQ4 (PIN NO. 11)	DQ1 (PIN NO. 14)	DQ2 (PIN NO. 13)
16	16	16	16
15 ◄────────0	15 ◄────────0	15 ◄────────0	15 ◄────────0

To determine the precise location on the die of a word in memory, reassign address numbers to the address pins as in the table below. The bit locations can then be determined directly from the bit map.

PIN NUMBER	REASSIGNED ADDRESS NUMBER	PIN NUMBER	REASSIGNED ADDRESS NUMBER
1	A6	6	A1
2	A5	7	A2
3	A4	15	$\overline{A9}$
4	A3	16	$\overline{A8}$
5	A0	17	$\overline{A7}$

 **MOTOROLA**

MC6821
(1.0 MHz)
MC68A21
(1.5 MHz)
MC68B21
(2.0 MHz)

PERIPHERAL INTERFACE ADAPTER (PIA)

The MC6821 Peripheral Interface Adapter provides the universal means of interfacing peripheral equipment to the M6800 family of microprocessors. This device is capable of interfacing the MPU to peripherals through two 8-bit bidirectional peripheral data buses and four control lines. No external logic is required for interfacing to most peripheral devices.

The functional configuration of the PIA is programmed by the MPU during system initialization. Each of the peripheral data lines can be programmed to act as an input or output, and each of the four control/interrupt lines may be programmed for one of several control modes. This allows a high degree of flexibility in the overall operation of the interface.

- 8-Bit Bidirectional Data Bus for Communication with the MPU
- Two Bidirectional 8-Bit Buses for Interface to Peripherals
- Two Programmable Control Registers
- Two Programmable Data Direction Registers
- Four Individually-Controlled Interrupt Input Lines; Two Usable as Peripheral Control Outputs
- Handshake Control Logic for Input and Output Peripheral Operation
- High-Impedance Three-State and Direct Transistor Drive Peripheral Lines
- Program Controlled Interrupt and Interrupt Disable Capability
- CMOS Drive Capability on Side A Peripheral Lines
- Two TTL Drive Capability on All A and B Side Buffers
- TTL-Compatible
- Static Operation

MOS

(N-CHANNEL, SILICON-GATE, DEPLETION LOAD)

PERIPHERAL INTERFACE ADAPTER

L SUFFIX
CERAMIC PACKAGE
CASE 715

S SUFFIX
CERDIP PACKAGE
CASE 734

P SUFFIX
PLASTIC PACKAGE
CASE 711

MAXIMUM RATINGS

Characteristics	Symbol	Value	Unit
Supply Voltage	V_{CC}	-0.3 to $+7.0$	V
Input Voltage	V_{in}	-0.3 to $+7.0$	V
Operating Temperature Range MC6821, MC68A21, MC68B21 MC6821C, MC68A21C, MC68B21C	T_A	T_L to T_H 0 to 70 -40 to $+85$	°C
Storage Temperature Range	T_{stg}	-55 to $+150$	°C

THERMAL CHARACTERISTICS

Characteristic	Symbol	Value	Unit
Thermal Resistance Ceramic Plastic Cerdip	θ_{JA}	50 100 60	°C/W

This device contains circuitry to protect the inputs against damage due to high static voltages or electric fields; however, it is advised that normal precautions be taken to avoid application of any voltage higher than maximum-rated voltages to this high-impedance circuit. Reliability of operation is enhanced if unused inputs are tied to an appropriate logic voltage (i.e., either V_{SS} or V_{CC}).

PIN ASSIGNMENT

V_{SS}	1	40	CA1
PA0	2	39	CA2
PA1	3	38	$\overline{IRQA}$
PA2	4	37	$\overline{IRQB}$
PA3	5	36	RS0
PA4	6	35	RS1
PA5	7	34	$\overline{RESET}$
PA6	8	33	D0
PA7	9	32	D1
PB0	10	31	D2
PB1	11	30	D3
PB2	12	29	D4
PB3	13	28	D5
PB4	14	27	D6
PB5	15	26	D7
PB6	16	25	E
PB7	17	24	CS1
CB1	18	23	$\overline{CS2}$
CB2	19	22	CS0
V_{CC}	20	21	$R/\overline{W}$

MC6821•MC68A21•MC68B21

POWER CONSIDERATIONS

The average chip-junction temperature, T_J, in °C can be obtained from:

$$T_J = T_A + (P_D \bullet \theta_{JA}) \tag{1}$$

Where:

T_A = Ambient Temperature, °C

θ_{JA} = Package Thermal Resistance, Junction-to-Ambient, °C/W

P_D = P_{INT} + P_{PORT}

P_{INT} = I_{CC} × V_{CC}, Watts — Chip Internal Power

P_{PORT} = Port Power Dissipation, Watts — User Determined

For most applications $P_{PORT} \blacktriangleleft P_{INT}$ and can be neglected. P_{PORT} may become significant if the device is configured to drive Darlington bases or sink LED loads.

An approximate relationship between P_D and T_J (if P_{PORT} is neglected) is:

$$P_D = K \div (T_J + 273°C) \tag{2}$$

Solving equations 1 and 2 for K gives:

$$K = P_D \bullet (T_A + 273°C) + \theta_{JA} \bullet P_D^2 \tag{3}$$

Where K is a constant pertaining to the particular part. K can be determined from equation 3 by measuring P_D (at equilibrium) for a known T_A. Using this value of K the values of P_D and T_J can be obtained by solving equations (1) and (2) iteratively for any value of T_A.

DC ELECTRICAL CHARACTERISTICS (V_{CC} = 5.0 Vdc ± 5%, V_{SS} = 0, T_A = T_L to T_H unless otherwise noted)

Characteristic		Symbol	Min	Typ	Max	Unit
BUS CONTROL INPUTS (R/$\overline{W}$, Enable, $\overline{RESET}$, RS0, RS1, CS0, CS1, CS2)						
Input High Voltage		V_{IH}	V_{SS} + 2.0	—	V_{CC}	V
Input Low Voltage		V_{IL}	V_{SS} - 0.3	—	V_{SS} + 0.8	V
Input Leakage Current (V_{in} = 0 to 5.25 V)		I_{in}	—	1.0	2.5	μA
Capacitance (V_{in} = 0, T_A = 25°C, f = 1.0 MHz)		C_{in}	—	—	7.5	pF
INTERRUPT OUTPUTS ($\overline{IRQA}$, $\overline{IRQB}$)						
Output Low Voltage (I_{Load} = 3.2 mA)		V_{OL}	—	—	V_{SS} + 0.4	V
Three-State Output Leakage Current		I_{OZ}	—	1.0	10	μA
Capacitance (V_{in} = 0, T_A = 25°C, f = 1.0 MHz)		C_{out}	—	—	5.0	pF
DATA BUS (D0-D7)						
Input High Voltage		V_{IH}	V_{SS} + 2.0	—	V_{CC}	V
Input Low Voltage		V_{IL}	V_{SS} - 0.3	—	V_{SS} + 0.8	V
Three-State Input Leakage Current (V_{in} = 0.4 to 2.4 V)		I_{IZ}	—	2.0	10	μA
Output High Voltage (I_{Load} = - 205 μA)		V_{OH}	V_{SS} + 2.4	—	—	V
Output Low Voltage (I_{Load} = 1.6 mA)		V_{OL}	—	—	V_{SS} + 0.4	V
Capacitance (V_{in} = 0, T_A = 25°C, f = 1.0 MHz)		C_{in}	—	—	12.5	pF
PERIPHERAL BUS (PA0-PA7, PB0-PB7, CA1, CA2, CB1, CB2)						
Input Leakage Current (V_{in} = 0 to 5.25 V)	R/$\overline{W}$, $\overline{RESET}$, RS0, RS1, CS0, CS1, $\overline{CS2}$, CA1, CB1, Enable	I_{in}	—	1.0	2.5	μA
Three-State Input Leakage Current (V_{in} = 0.4 to 2.4 V)	PB0-PB7, CB2	I_{IZ}	—	2.0	10	μA
Input High Current (V_{IH} = 2.4 V)	PA0-PA7, CA2	I_{IH}	- 200	- 400	—	μA
Darlington Drive Current (V_O = 1.5 V)	PB0-PB7, CB2	I_{OH}	- 1.0	—	- 10	mA
Input Low Current (V_{IL} = 0.4 V)	PA0-PA7, CA2	I_{IL}	—	- 1.3	- 2.4	mA
Output High Voltage (I_{Load} = - 200 μA) (I_{Load} = - 10 μA)	PA0-PA7, PB0-PB7, CA2, CB2 PA0-PA7, CA2	V_{OH}	V_{SS} + 2.4 V_{CC} - 1.0	— —	— —	V
Output Low Voltage (I_{Load} = 3.2 mA)		V_{OL}	—	—	V_{SS} + 0.4	V
Capacitance (V_{in} = 0, T_A = 25°C, f = 1.0 MHz)		C_{in}	—	—	10	pF
POWER REQUIREMENTS						
Internal Power Dissipation (Measured at T_A = T_L)		P_{INT}	—	—	550	mW

BUS TIMING CHARACTERISTICS (See Notes 1 and 2).

Ident. Number	Characteristic	Symbol	MC6821		MC68A21		MC68B21		Unit
			Min	Max	Min	Max	Min	Max	
1	Cycle Time	t_{cyc}	1.0	10	0.67	10	0.5	10	μS
2	Pulse Width, E Low	PW_{EL}	430	–	280	–	210	–	ns
3	Pulse Width, E High	PW_{EH}	450	–	280	–	220	–	ns
4	Clock Rise and Fall Time	t_r, t_f	–	25	–	25	–	20	ns
9	Address Hold Time	t_{AH}	10	–	10	–	10	–	ns
13	Address Setup Time Before E	t_{AS}	80	–	60	–	40	–	ns
14	Chip Select Setup Time Before E	t_{CS}	80	–	60	–	40	–	ns
15	Chip Select Hold Time	t_{CH}	10	–	10	–	10	–	ns
18	Read Data Hold Time	t_{DHR}	20	100	20	100	20	100	ns
21	Write Data Hold Time	t_{DHW}	10	–	10	–	10	–	ms
30	Output Data Delay Time	t_{DDR}	–	290	–	180	–	150	ns
31	Input Data Setup Time	t_{DSW}	165	–	80	–	60	–	ns

FIGURE 1 — BUS TIMING

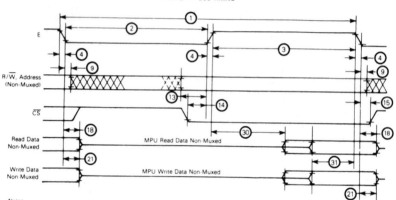

Notes:
1. Voltage levels shown are $V_L \leq 0.4$ V, $V_H \geq 2.4$ V, unless otherwise specified.
2. Measurement points shown are 0.8 V and 2.0 V, unless otherwise specified.

MC6821•MC68A21•MC68B21

PERIPHERAL TIMING CHARACTERISTICS ($V_{CC} = 5.0$ V ±5%, $V_{SS} = 0$ V, $T_A = T_L$ to T_H unless otherwise specified)

Characteristic	Symbol	MC6821		MC68A21		MC68B21		Unit	Reference Fig. No.
		Min	Max	Min	Max	Min	Max		
Data Setup Time	t_{PDS}	200	–	135	–	100	–	ns	6
Data Hold Time	t_{PDH}	0	–	0	–	0	–	ns	6
Delay Time, Enable Negative Transition to CA2 Negative Transition	t_{CA2}	–	1.0	–	0.670	–	0.500	μs	3, 7, 8
Delay Time, Enable Negative Transition to CA2 Positive Transition	T_{RS1}	–	1.0	–	0.670	–	0.500	μs	3, 7
Rise and Fall Times for CA1 and CA2 Input Signals	t_r, t_f	–	1.0	–	1.0	–	1.0	μs	8
Delay Time from CA1 Active Transition to CA2 Positive Transition	t_{RS2}	–	2.0	–	1.35	–	1.0	μs	3, 8
Delay Time, Enable Negative Transition to Data Valid	t_{PDW}	–	1.0	–	0.670	–	0.5	μs	3, 9, 10
Delay Time, Enable Negative Transition to CMOS Data Valid PA0-PA7, CA2	t_{CMOS}	–	2.0	–	1.35	–	1.0	μs	4, 9
Delay Time, Enable Positive Transition to CB2 Negative Transition	t_{CB2}	–	1.0	–	0.670	–	0.5	μs	3, 11, 12
Delay Time, Data Valid to CB2 Negative Transition	t_{DC}	20	–	20	–	20	–	ns	3, 10
Delay Time, Enable Positive Transition to CB2 Positive Transition	t_{RS1}	–	1.0	–	0.670	–	0.5	μs	3, 11
Control Output Pulse Width, CA2/CB2	PW_{CT}	500	–	375	–	250	–	ns	3, 11
Rise and Fall Time for CB1 and CB2 Input Signals	t_r, t_f	–	1.0	–	1.0	–	1.0	μ	12
Delay Time, CB1 Active Transition to CB2 Positive Transition	t_{RS2}	–	2.0	–	1.35	–	1.0	μs	3, 12
Interrupt Release Time, $\overline{IRQA}$ and $\overline{IRQB}$	t_{IR}	–	1.60	–	1.10	–	0.85	μs	5, 14
Interrupt Response Time	t_{RS3}	–	1.0	–	1.0	–	1.0	μs	5, 13
Interrupt Input Pulse Time	PW_i	500	–	500	–	500	–	ns	13
$\overline{RESET}$ Low Time*	t_{RL}	1.0	–	0.66	–	0.5	–	μs	15

*The $\overline{RESET}$ line must be high a minimum of 1.0 μs before addressing the PIA.

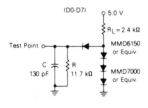

FIGURE 2 — BUS TIMING TEST LOADS

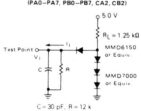

FIGURE 3 — TTL EQUIVALENT TEST LOAD

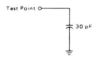

FIGURE 4 — CMOS EQUIVALENT TEST LOAD

FIGURE 5 — NMOS EQUIVALENT TEST LOAD

MC6821•MC68A21•MC68B21

FIGURE 6 — PERIPHERAL DATA SETUP AND HOLD TIMES
(Read Mode)

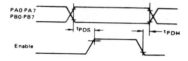

FIGURE 7 — CA2 DELAY TIME
(Read Mode; CRA-5 = CRA3 = 1, CRA-4 = 0)

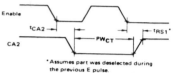

*Assumes part was deselected during
the previous E pulse.

FIGURE 8 — CA2 DELAY TIME
(Read Mode; CRA-5 = 1, CRA-3 = CRA-4 = 0)

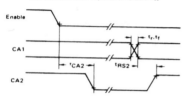

FIGURE 9 — PERIPHERAL CMOS DATA DELAY TIMES
(Write Mode; CRA-5 = CRA-3 = 1, CRA-4 = 0)

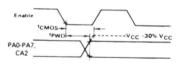

FIGURE 10 — PERIPHERAL DATA AND CB2 DELAY TIMES
(Write Mode; CRB-5 = CRB-3 = 1, CRB-4 = 0)

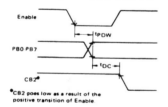

*CB2 goes low as a result of the
positive transition of Enable.

FIGURE 11 — CB2 DELAY TIME
(Write Mode; CRB-5 = CRB-3 = 1, CRB-4 = 0)

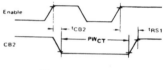

*Assumes part was deselected during the
previous E pulse

FIGURE 12 — CB2 DELAY TIME
(Write Mode; CRB-5 = 1, CRB-3 = CRB-4 = 0)

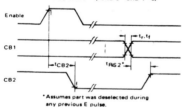

*Assumes part was deselected during
any previous E pulse.

FIGURE 13 — INTERRUPT PULSE WIDTH AND $\overline{\text{IRQ}}$ RESPONSE

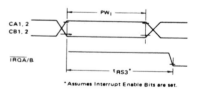

*Assumes Interrupt Enable Bits are set.

Note: Timing measurements are referenced to and from a low voltage of 0.8 volts and a high voltage of 2.0 volts, unless otherwise noted.

MC6821•MC68A21•MC68B21

FIGURE 14 — IRQ RELEASE TIME

FIGURE 15 — RESET LOW TIME

*The RESET line must be a V_{IH} for a minimum of 1.0 μs before addressing the PIA.

Note: Timing measurements are referenced to and from a low voltage of 0.8 volts and a high voltage of 2.0 volts, unless otherwise noted.

FIGURE 16 — EXPANDED BLOCK DIAGRAM

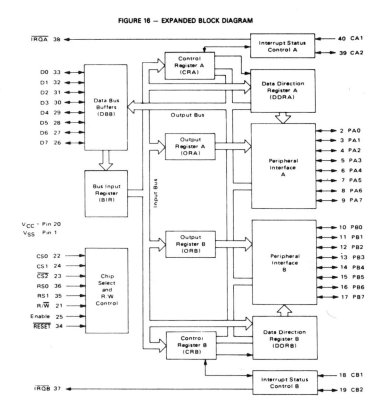

MC6821•MC68A21•MC68B21

PIA INTERFACE SIGNALS FOR MPU

The PIA interfaces to the M6800 bus with an 8-bit bidirectional data bus, three chip select lines, two register select lines, two interrupt request lines, a read/write line, an enable line and a reset line. To ensure proper operation with the MC6800, MC6802, or MC6808 microprocessors, VMA should be used as an active part of the address decoding.

Bidirectional Data (D0-D7) — The bidirectional data lines (D0-D7) allow the transfer of data between the MPU and the PIA. The data bus output drivers are three-state devices that remain in the high-impedance (off) state except when the MPU performs a PIA read operation. The read/write line is in the read (high) state when the PIA is selected for a read operation.

Enable (E) — The enable pulse, E, is the only timing signal that is supplied to the PIA. Timing of all other signals is referenced to the leading and trailing edges of the E pulse.

Read/Write (R/W̄) — This signal is generated by the MPU to control the direction of data transfers on the data bus. A low state on the PIA read/write line enables the input buffers and data is transferred from the MPU to the PIA on the E signal if the device has been selected. A high on the read/write line sets up the PIA for a transfer of data to the bus. The PIA output buffers are enabled when the proper address and the enable pulse E are present.

RESET — The active low RESET line is used to reset all register bits in the PIA to a logical zero (low). This line can be used as a power-on reset and as a master reset during system operation.

Chip Selects (CS0, CS1, and C̄S̄2̄) — These three input signals are used to select the PIA. CS0 and CS1 must be high and C̄S̄2̄ must be low for selection of the device. Data transfers are then performed under the control of the enable and read/write signals. The chip select lines must be stable

for the duration of the E pulse. The device is deselected when any of the chip selects are in the inactive state.

Register Selects (RS0 and RS1) — The two register select lines are used to select the various registers inside the PIA. These two lines are used in conjunction with internal Control Registers to select a particular register that is to be written or read.

The register and chip select lines should be stable for the duration of the E pulse while in the read or write cycle.

Interrupt Request (ĪR̄Q̄Ā and ĪR̄Q̄B̄) — The active low Interrupt Request lines (ĪR̄Q̄Ā and ĪR̄Q̄B̄) act to interrupt the MPU either directly or through interrupt priority circuitry. These lines are "open drain" (no load device on the chip). This permits all interrupt request lines to be tied together in a wire-OR configuration.

Each Interrupt Request line has two internal interrupt flag bits that can cause the Interrupt Request line to go low. Each flag bit is associated with a particular peripheral interrupt line. Also, four interrupt enable bits are provided in the PIA which may be used to inhibit a particular interrupt from a peripheral device.

Servicing an interrupt by the MPU may be accomplished by a software routine that, on a prioritized basis, sequentially reads and tests the two control registers in each PIA for interrupt flag bits that are set.

The interrupt flags are cleared (zeroed) as a result of an MPU Read Peripheral Data Operation of the corresponding data register. After being cleared, an interrupt flag bit cannot be enabled to be set until the PIA is deselected during an E pulse. The E pulse is used to condition the interrupt control lines (CA1, CA2, CB1, CB2). When these lines are used as interrupt inputs, at least one E pulse must occur from the inactive edge to the active edge of the interrupt input signal to condition the edge sense network. If the interrupt flag has been enabled and the edge sense circuit has been properly conditioned, the interrupt flag will be set on the next active transition of the interrupt input pin.

PIA PERIPHERAL INTERFACE LINES

The PIA provides two 8-bit bidirectional data buses and four interrupt/control lines for interfacing to peripheral devices.

Section A Peripheral Data (PA0-PA7) — Each of the peripheral data lines can be programmed to act as an input or output. This is accomplished by setting a "1" in the corresponding Data Direction Register bit for those lines which are to be outputs. A "0" in a bit of the Data Direction Register causes the corresponding peripheral data line to act as an input. During an MPU Read Peripheral Data Operation, the data on peripheral lines programmed to act as inputs appears directly on the corresponding MPU Data Bus lines. In the input mode, the internal pullup resistor on these lines represents a maximum of 1.5 standard TTL loads.

The data in Output Register A will appear on the data lines that are programmed to be outputs. A logical "1" written into the register will cause a "high" on the corresponding data

line while a "0" results in a "low." Data in Output Register A may be read by an MPU "Read Peripheral Data A" operation when the corresponding lines are programmed as outputs. This data will be read property if the voltage on the peripheral data lines is greater than 2.0 volts for a logic "1" output and less than 0.8 volt for a logic "0" output. Loading the output lines such that the voltage on these lines does not reach full voltage causes the data transferred into the MPU on a Read operation to differ from that contained in the respective bit of Output Register A.

Section B Peripheral Data (PB0-PB7) — The peripheral data lines in the B Section of the PIA can be programmed to act as either inputs or outputs in a similar manner to PA0-PA7. They have three-state capability, allowing them to enter a high-impedance state when the peripheral data line is used as an input. In addition, data on the peripheral data lines

MC6821•MC68A21•MC68B21

PB0-PB7 will be read properly from those lines programmed as outputs even if the voltages are below 2.0 volts for a "high" or above 0.8 V for a "low". As outputs, these lines are compatible with standard TTL and may also be used as a source of up to 1 milliampere at 1.5 volts to directly drive the base of a transistor switch.

Interrupt Input (CA1 and CB1) — Peripheral input lines CA1 and CB1 are input only lines that set the interrupt flags of the control registers. The active transition for these signals is also programmed by the two control registers.

Peripheral Control (CA2) — The peripheral control line CA2 can be programmed to act as an interrupt input or as a peripheral control output. As an output, this line is compatible with standard TTL; as an input the internal pullup resistor on this line represents 1.5 standard TTL loads. The function of this signal line is programmed with Control Register A.

Peripheral Control (CB2) — Peripheral Control line CB2 may also be programmed to act as an interrupt input or peripheral control output. As an input, this line has high input impedance and is compatible with standard TTL. As an output it is compatible with standard TTL and may also be used as a source of up to 1 milliampere at 1.5 volts to directly drive the base of a transistor switch. This line is programmed by Control Register B.

INTERNAL CONTROLS

INITIALIZATION

A RESET has the effect of zeroing all PIA registers. This will set PA0-PA7, PB0-PB7, CA2 and CB2 as inputs, and all interrupts disabled. The PIA must be configured during the restart program which follows the reset.

There are six locations within the PIA accessible to the MPU data bus: two Peripheral Registers, two Data Direction Registers, and two Control Registers. Selection of these locations is controlled by the RS0 and RS1 inputs together with bit 2 in the Control Register, as shown in Table 1.

Details of possible configurations of the Data Direction and Control Register are as follows:

TABLE 1 – INTERNAL ADDRESSING

RS1	RS0	Control Register Bit CRA-2	CRB-2	Location Selected
0	0	1	X	Peripheral Register A
0	0	0	X	Data Direction Register A
0	1	X	X	Control Register A
1	0	X	1	Peripheral Register B
1	0	X	0	Data Direction Register B
1	1	X	X	Control Register B

X Don't Care

PORT A-B HARDWARE CHARACTERISTICS

As shown in Figure 17, the MC6821 has a pair of I/O ports whose characteristics differ greatly. The A side is designed to drive CMOS logic to normal 30% to 70% levels, and incorporates an internal pullup device that remains connected even in the input mode. Because of this, the A side requires more drive current in the input mode than Port B. In contrast, the B side uses a normal three-state NMOS buffer which cannot pullup to CMOS levels without external resistors. The B side can drive extra loads such as Darlingtons without problem. When the PIA comes out of reset, the A port represents inputs with pullup resistors, whereas the B side (input mode also) will float high or low, depending upon the load connected to it.

Notice the differences between a Port A and Port B read operation when in the output mode. When reading Port A, the actual pin is read, whereas the B side read comes from an output latch, ahead of the actual pin.

CONTROL REGISTERS (CRA and CRB)

The two Control Registers (CRA and CRB) allow the MPU to control the operation of the four peripheral control lines CA1, CA2, CB1, and CB2. In addition they allow the MPU to enable the interrupt lines and monitor the status of the interrupt flags. Bits 0 through 5 of the two registers may be written or read by the MPU when the proper chip select and register select signals are applied. Bits 6 and 7 of the two registers are read only and are modified by external interrupts occurring on control lines CA1, CA2, CB1, or CB2. The format of the control words is shown in Figure 18.

DATA DIRECTION ACCESS CONTROL BIT (CRA-2 and CRB-2)

Bit 2, in each Control Register (CRA and CRB), determines selection of either a Peripheral Output Register or the corresponding Data Direction E Register when the proper register select signals are applied to RS0 and RS1. A "1" in bit 2 allows access of the Peripheral Interface Register, while a "0" causes the Data Direction Register to be addressed.

Interrupt Flags (CRA-6, CRA-7, CRB-6, and CRB-7) — The four interrupt flag bits are set by active transitions of signals on the four Interrupt and Peripheral Control lines when those lines are programmed to be inputs. These bits cannot be set directly from the MPU Data Bus and are reset indirectly by a Read Peripheral Data Operation on the appropriate section.

Control of CA2 and CB2 Peripheral Control Lines (CRA-3, CRA-4, CRA-5, CRB-3, CRB-4, and CRB-5) — Bits 3, 4, and 5 of the two control registers are used to control the CA2 and CB2 Peripheral Control lines. These bits determine if the control lines will be an interrupt input or an output control signal. If bit CRA-5 (CRB-5) is low, CA2 (CB2) is an interrupt input line similar to CA1 (CB1). When CRA-5 (CRB-5) is high, CA2 (CB2) becomes an output signal that may be used to control peripheral data transfers. When in the output mode, CA2 and CB2 have slightly different loading characteristics.

MC6821•MC68A21•MC68B21

Control of CA1 and CB1 Interrupt Input Lines (CRA-0, CRB-1, CRA-1, and CRB-1) — The two lowest-order bits of the control registers are used to control the interrupt input lines CA1 and CB1. Bits CRA-0 and CRB-0 are used to enable the MPU interrupt signals $\overline{IRQA}$ and $\overline{IRQB}$, respectively. Bits CRA-1 and CRB-1 determine the active transition of the interrupt input signals CA1 and CB1.

FIGURE 17 — PORT A AND PORT B EQUIVALENT CIRCUITS

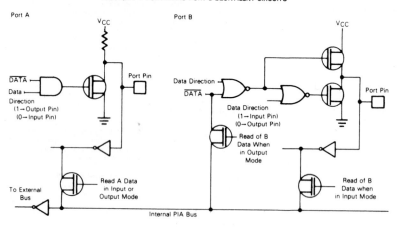

MC6821•MC68A21•MC68B21

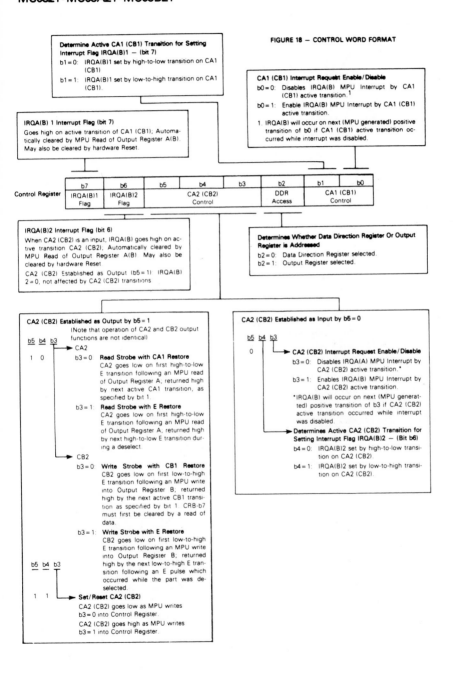

FIGURE 18 — CONTROL WORD FORMAT

Determine Active CA1 (CB1) Transition for Setting Interrupt Flag IRQA(B)1 — (bit 7)
b1 = 0:   IRQA(B)1 set by high-to-low transition on CA1 (CB1)
b1 = 1:   IRQA(B)1 set by low-to-high transition on CA1 (CB1).

CA1 (CB1) Interrupt Request Enable/Disable
b0 = 0:   Disables IRQA(B) MPU Interrupt by CA1 (CB1) active transition.[1]
b0 = 1:   Enable IRQA(B) MPU Interrupt by CA1 (CB1) active transition.
1. IRQA(B) will occur on next (MPU generated) positive transition of b0 if CA1 (CB1) active transition occurred while interrupt was disabled.

IRQA(B) 1 Interrupt Flag (bit 7)
Goes high on active transition of CA1 (CB1); Automatically cleared by MPU Read of Output Register A(B). May also be cleared by hardware Reset.

	b7	b6	b5	b4	b3	b2	b1	b0
Control Register	IRQA(B)1 Flag	IRQA(B)2 Flag		CA2 (CB2) Control		DDR Access	CA1 (CB1) Control	

IRQA(B)2 Interrupt Flag (bit 6)
When CA2 (CB2) is an input, IRQA(B) goes high on active transition CA2 (CB2), Automatically cleared by MPU Read of Output Register A(B). May also be cleared by hardware Reset
CA2 (CB2) Established as Output (b5 = 1) IRQA(B) 2 = 0, not affected by CA2 (CB2) transitions

Determines Whether Data Direction Register Or Output Register is Addressed
b2 = 0:   Data Direction Register selected.
b2 = 1:   Output Register selected.

CA2 (CB2) Established as Output by b5 = 1
(Note that operation of CA2 and CB2 output functions are not identical)

b5	b4	b3	
1	0		► CA2

b3 = 0:   **Read Strobe with CA1 Restore**
CA2 goes low on first high-to-low E transition following an MPU read of Output Register A; returned high by next active CA1 transition, as specified by bit 1.

b3 = 1:   **Read Strobe with E Restore**
CA2 goes low on first high-to-low E transition following an MPU read of Output Register A; returned high by next high-to-low E transition during a deselect.

► CB2

b3 = 0:   **Write Strobe with CB1 Restore**
CB2 goes low on first low-to-high E transition following an MPU write into Output Register B; returned high by the next active CB1 transition as specified by bit 1. CRB-b7 must first be cleared by a read of data.

b3 = 1:   **Write Strobe with E Restore**
CB2 goes low on first low-to-high E transition following an MPU write into Output Register B; returned high by the next low-to-high E transition following an E pulse which occurred while the part was deselected.

b5	b4	b3	
1	1		► **Set/Reset CA2 (CB2)**

CA2 (CB2) goes low as MPU writes b3 = 0 into Control Register.
CA2 (CB2) goes high as MPU writes b3 = 1 into Control Register.

CA2 (CB2) Established as Input by b5 = 0

b5	b4	b3
0		

► **CA2 (CB2) Interrupt Request Enable/Disable**
b3 = 0:   Disables IRQA(B) MPU Interrupt by CA2 (CB2) active transition.*
b3 = 1:   Enables IRQA(B) MPU Interrupt by CA2 (CB2) active transition.
*IRQA(B) will occur on next (MPU generated) positive transition of b3 if CA2 (CB2) active transition occurred while interrupt was disabled.

► **Determines Active CA2 (CB2) Transition for Setting Interrupt Flag IRQA(B)2 — (Bit b6)**
b4 = 0:   IRQA(B)2 set by high-to-low transition on CA2 (CB2).
b4 = 1:   IRQA(B)2 set by low-to-high transition on CA2 (CB2).

INDEX

A

AO logical address, 7–8
$\overline{\text{AS}}$ control line, 8
Address stimulus, SST, 104
Address buffering, 10, 11
Address buffers, verifying, 114–118
Address bus, overview, 6–9

B

Bidirectional buffering, 15–20
Bidirectional buffer, 74LS245, 18
Bidirectional buffer, schematic, 21
Bidirectional buffer, schematic diagram, 117
Block diagram of ROM system, 23, 24
Block diagram of Static RAM, 35
Buffer, bidirectional 74LS245, 18
Buffering, bidirectional, 15–20

C

Chip select for the 6821, 80–82
Common I/O RAM, 38–44
Connecting the 68000 address bus to the 6821, 80
Connecting the 68000 to the 6821 data bus, 79, 80
Control line stimulus, SST, 106–108
Control line, $\overline{\text{AS}}$, 8
Control line, $\overline{\text{IORQ}}$, 60
Control line, $\overline{\text{LDS}}$, 12

M

O

P

R

U

$\overline{\text{UDS}}$ control line, 12
$\overline{\text{UDS}}$, timing diagram, 20
Upper data strobe, 12

V

VPA output of 68000, 82–84
Verification of $\overline{\text{DTACK}}$, SST, 124, 125
Verify the port select, SST, 148, 149
Verifying the address buffers, 114–118
Verifying the memory select lines, 120–122
Visually monitor $\overline{\text{DTACK}}$, 159

W

Write access time, extending, 51–54